Philadelphia's
Outdoor Art

Updated and Expanded

Philadelphia's
Outdoor Art

A WALKING TOUR, 3RD EDITION

Roslyn F. Brenner

Camino Books, Inc.
Philadelphia

Manufactured in the United States of America

1 2 3 4 5   05 04 03 02

Library of Congress Cataloging-in-Publication Data

Brenner, Roslyn F.
   Philadelphia's outdoor art : a walking tour / Roslyn F. Brenner—3rd ed.
        p.   cm.
   ISBN 0-940159-72-4
   1. Outdoor sculpture—Pennsylvania—Philadelphia—Guidebooks. 2. Philadelphia (Pa.)—Guidebooks.
I. Title.
   NB235.P44 B74 2002
   730'.9748'11—dc21   2002001742

Cover and interior design: Jerilyn Kauffman
Maps by John Gummere

This book is available at a special discount on bulk purchases for promotional, business, and educational use. For information write to:

Publisher
Camino Books, Inc.
P.O. Box 59026
Philadelphia, PA 19102

www.caminobooks.com

CONTENTS

PREFACE

Every day we rush past our silent monuments, seeing them either as familiar landmarks or as friends we can count on to be there, or not seeing them at all. Some of them have been around for so long that we forget who they honor, and some are so new that we are not sure we even know them.

This book is a walking tour of Philadelphia's outdoor sculptures, many of which are located along the Benjamin Franklin Parkway. This beautiful boulevard has such an array of public artworks that it is truly a "museum without walls." We do not attempt to evaluate the works as art objects, but concentrate instead on answering why, when and how they came to be. We are including, in this edition of the book, the sculptures on Kelly Drive, a road that meets the Parkway at the Philadelphia Museum of Art and continues along the Schuylkill River.

In the past, monuments were unveiled amid great crowds and festivities. Today, it seems, they appear overnight and without fanfare. It is a wonder, however, that they exist at all because today, as in the past, there are constant furors over selections, location and maintenance. Art juries and the public, as well as the artists themselves, are quick to criticize each other over every new piece.

The director of the Philadelphia Museum of Art was once quoted as saying that she believes that, given time, even the most modernistic of Philadelphia's public sculp-

ture will slip comfortably into the same general acceptance enjoyed by masterpieces of the past, adding, "I think people will come to find them a very intimate part of their lives."

The groups of people who have promoted and funded these monuments are emotional about them and gratified by their presence. For our purposes, however, it is more important to gain a wider appreciation of Philadelphia's outdoor art and its often fascinating history.

Three groups are intimately involved and ultimately responsible for our public artworks. The similarity of their names sometimes leads to confusion about their separate identities.

The Philadelphia Art Commission

The mayor appoints nine members to serve on the Art Commission without pay. The nine members are usually distinguished citizens from the professional and business world who are interested in the arts, and they include at least one artist and one representative of city government (usually the Commissioner of Public Property).

The Art Commission is responsible for the approval of all works of art acquired by the city, and for their locations. It has to approve the designs of all buildings that are paid for wholly or partially by the city. It also must examine any structure for which the city or a public authority supplies the site, and anything to be erected in a public place.

The Art Commission is required by law to tour the city's statues semiannually and report on their condition to the Commissioner of Public Property. They once recommended that all bronzes should be washed down with a strong detergent and covered with wax twice a year!

In 1959 the City Council passed an ordinance which required that one percent of the construction costs of major new public buildings be reserved for the purchase of fine art. The Art Commission sees to it that this ordinance is adhered to, a task that greatly increases its responsibilities.

The Fairmount Park Commission

In 1867 the General Assembly of Pennsylvania passed a special act to authorize the City of Philadelphia to buy land for Fairmount Park, which was to be designed and maintained forever as an open public place. The Fairmount Park Commission was established to oversee the development and management of the park. It is composed of ten citizens appointed for five-year terms by the Board of Judges of the Common Pleas Courts and six *ex officio* members of city government. Its original members were prestigious citizens of fine character, and through the years people of good reputation have been chosen to serve without pay. In addition, there are salaried officers who direct the day-to-day operations of maintenance and engineering for Fairmount and 25 other small parks and squares, as well as the Benjamin Franklin Parkway and Roosevelt Boulevard.

The early years in the development of Fairmount Park were taken up with buying land and properties, planting trees, designing gardens and creating play areas for water sports and baseball. It eventually grew to be the largest in-city park in the world.

At one time the Park Commission was given the power to employ a force of Park Guards. They traveled around on foot or on bicycles as well as on horseback and in patrol cars. Park maintenance was exemplary during that time, but the guards have been disbanded, and today the Philadelphia Police Department has assumed responsibility for the park grounds. The Park Commission has had to battle vandalism, which causes thousands of dollars in damage each year. But for those few who don't appreciate the beauty of Fairmount Park, there are millions who are grateful for it.

The Fairmount Park Art Association

In 1871, a few years after the Park Commission began its work, a group of civic leaders, spearheaded by Charles H. Howell and Henry K. Fox, created the Fairmount Park Art Association to help beautify the city with "fruits of the spirit." They planned to raise funds to ensure that fine works of art would be placed in the new park "to add man-made beauty to God's and as a reaction against the excessive spirit of industrialization in Philadelphia, which had condemned it to be a workshop and nothing more." Anthony Drexel, the founder of Drexel University, was the Art Association's first president, holding that post from 1872 to 1893. Over the years the group has acquired more than 100 works of sculpture for display to the public.

The Art Association recently took on the job of cleaning the outdoor monuments and is now in the process of cataloging all the works. A major reason for all this attention is that "no other city in the United States, and few in the world, can boast of so rich and varied a heritage of outdoor public sculpture as Philadelphia."

ACKNOWLEDGMENTS

It is said, "Ask and ye shall receive." I did not realize how much I would need to ask or how generous and forthcoming people would be.

Again, I am deeply indebted to Regina Tuzio for her indispensable help and calmness in the crunch, to Allan Kalish for his continuing interest, to Frank Donahue of the *Philadelphia Inquirer* library, to the patient librarians in the Art Department of the Philadelphia Free Library, to Jessica Senker of the Office of Arts and Culture of the Philadelphia Art Commission, who has been attentive and encouraging, to the editors of *Where* magazine for permitting me to reproduce my material, to the Fairmount Park Art Association and the Fairmount Park Commission Archives, to the staff of the Urban Archives at Temple University, to the Philadelphia Athenaeum and the Academy of Natural Sciences, to Pepi and Joel Bloom for their friendly assistance, and to Rebecca Hofman for her speedy word processing.

I am especially grateful to my husband, Cliff Brenner, for his organizing ability, skillful editing and constant inspiration.

My sincere thanks to all.

Roslyn F. Brenner

The Benjamin Franklin Parkway and Environs

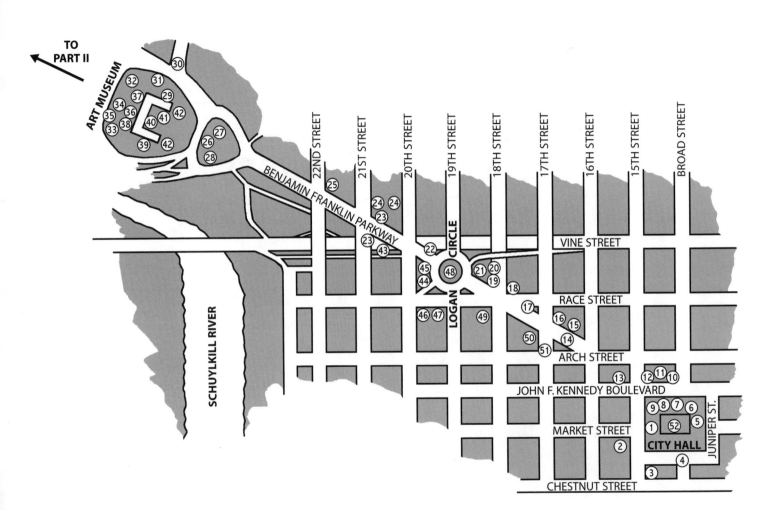

PART I   THE BENJAMIN FRANKLIN PARKWAY AND ENVIRONS

1

As we start our tour these words seem
appropriate:

"Art gives a man something to feed his soul and
whether he lives in a garret or a marble palace,
he can enjoy the works in public display."

We begin in the west plaza of City Hall with
Emlen Etting's Phoenix Rising.

Aluminum covered with baked enamel
Height: 20′
Base: reinforced concrete

Richardson Dilworth Plaza
Unveiled November 4, 1982

Phoenix Rising

EMLEN ETTING

In 1977 the administration presiding in City Hall named its west plaza for Richardson Dilworth. It was then that a Friends of Dilworth Committee was formed to raise funds for a work of art to be erected in his memory. Richardson Dilworth, the colorful mayor of Philadelphia (1956–62) and later the president of the city's Board of Education (1967–72), had also served as City Treasurer and District Attorney. During Dilworth's time in office many innovative programs in urban renewal were begun, and as always, when changes are suggested, there were quarrels and power struggles. However, no one doubted the Pittsburgh native's love for his adopted city.

In 1982 the abstract sculpture *Phoenix Rising* was finished. It was designed, according to sculptor Emlen Etting, to "symbolize Dilworth's idea of a Philadelphia renaissance." When it was unveiled, several hundred of Dilworth's friends and relatives and many political personalities came. Some critics ridiculed the sculptor, but perhaps it is fitting that a man whose career was filled with courage and controversy should have a prominently displayed memorial that stands proudly in the midst of disagreements.

Emlen Etting was a native Philadelphian and has works in major collections throughout the world.

2 *We turn to walk to* The Clothespin, *which stands ready to clip together the old and the new.*

Corten steel
Height: 45'
Weight: 10 tons
Base: concrete

Centre Square Plaza, 15th and Market Streets
Installed July 1, 1976

The Clothespin

CLAES OLDENBURG

Jack Wolgin, a businessman who was instrumental in bringing *The Clothespin* to Philadelphia, was enthusiastic about the city's new outdoor sculpture: "Do you realize that 30,000 to 40,000 people a day will see these fantastic works of art? That number would never go to a museum." The day it was installed, *Philadelphia Inquirer* art critic Victoria Donahue commented, "The clothespin halves meet and lock together with a large loopspring embrace."

The sculptor, Claes Oldenburg, liked old-fashioned wooden clothespins, and he happened to be playing with one while in an airplane flying over Chicago. He noticed that the buildings below looked the same size as the clothespin he was holding; that gave him the idea to design skyscrapers in the shape of colossal clothespins. When he created this sculpture he said that a clothespin is something that everyone can relate to, but that "this is more than a clothespin, it is my own design with a gothic look and elegance in its sweeping curves."

Oldenburg is often inspired by objects that are taken for granted in everyday life, and sometimes his work produces outraged reactions. In 1969, his giant *Lipstick* practically caused a riot on the Yale University campus. Oldenburg's defense was that "I am drawn by sympathy to those parts of nature that are neglected in an attitude of conventional seriousness."

The director of the Philadelphia Museum of Art, Anne d'Harnoncourt, once observed that "in a sense, a work of art often demands a struggle of some kind to understand it." But perhaps we should quote the person who, in passing by *The Clothespin*, was heard to say, "Centre Square needs some humor!"

3

Across 15th Street The Triune *swirls above the maelstrom of traffic.*

Polished bronze
Height: 22'
Weight: 30,000 lbs.
Base: concrete (6'6")

15th Street and South Penn Square
Installed March 1975

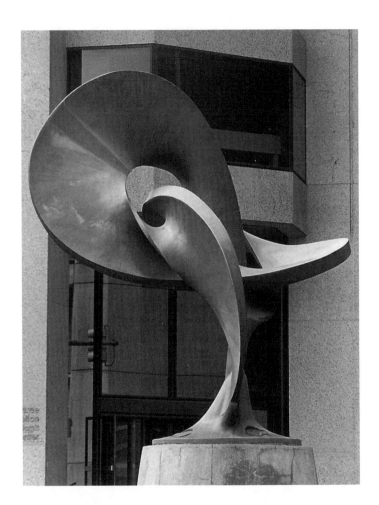

The Triune

ROBERT ENGMAN

People on the street say they like *The Triune* because it looks "different from all angles." Some compare it to a pretzel. According to sculptor Robert Engman, "If it simply gives people cause to wonder, it will have accomplished its primary objective. Sculpture . . . provides a visual experience. The name and the work itself symbolize the collaborative efforts of industry, people and government to accomplish something inspirational and enduring."

In 1968, Engman was a professor of graduate studies in sculpture at the University of Pennsylvania when the mayor appointed him to the city art commission board. In 1972, when he was fired from that board by a different mayor, he remarked, "I don't think he [the mayor] would know art if he fell over it. This [dismissal] was politically inspired by people who are complete visual illiterates."

In that same year, Engman became co-chairman of the art department at Penn's Graduate School of Fine Arts and he also started work on *The Triune*. For three years he and an assistant worked in an old industrial shed. They used electric-powered grinding wheels to smooth the foundry finish of the huge castings. *The Triune* was given to the city by two of its largest banks.

4 *Following the direction of the traffic we come to President McKinley, whose favorite buttonhole flower, the scarlet carnation, was adopted in his honor as the state flower of his native Ohio.*

Bronze
Height: 9½'
Base: granite (14½')

South Plaza, City Hall
Installed 1908

William McKinley

CHARLES ALBERT LOPEZ AND ISADOR KONTI

William McKinley is credited with being the first president to open the White House to newspapermen, although it was his secretary who met with them every evening for a discussion of the day's events. McKinley is also quoted as announcing, "I hold that labor gets on best when capital gets on best and that capital gets on best when labor is paid the most."

After an anarchist assassinated the president in 1901, the *Philadelphia Inquirer* initiated a public subscription for a monument. School children alone contributed $32,000. In 1902 the Fairmount Park Association opened a design competition and Charles Albert Lopez won out over 38 other entrants. His work, however, was slowed by those in charge who insisted on changes in the original design. He died before it was completed, and Isador Konti was asked to finish it.

McKinley is shown in a characteristic pose, delivering an oration. Below him sits a symbolic figure of Wisdom instructing Youth. According to the official dedication pamphlet, the lower group of figures "takes away the stiffness of the single figure, adds womanly beauty and childish innocence and results in a composition which is singularly pleasing to the untutored as well as to the learned student of art."

In 1953 a furor arose when the statue was painted with an artificial finish to repair the damage to the natural patina caused by sandblasting. A city councilman demanded that the workmen stop "the desecration," but the Art Commission saw to it that the job was done.

5 *Now continue around City Hall to the spot where*
John Wanamaker watches the world go by.
John Massey Rhind, the sculptor of this work,
also did the statue of Stephen Girard at the
Philadelphia Museum of Art.

Bronze
Height: 8½′
Base: granite (7′)

East Plaza, City Hall
Installed November 29, 1923

John Wanamaker

JOHN MASSEY RHIND

It took fifteen years to pay for the monument to President McKinley, but it took less than three months to finance the Wanamaker memorial. A great popular movement began with contributions from children in Sunday schools, public and private schools, and from private citizens. The school children alone donated $50,000 worth of pennies.

The John Wanamaker Memorial Committee commissioned John Massey Rhind to do the statue, which they presented as a gift to the city. (John Rhind's father, a Scottish builder, once employed a young stone-cutter who later became the sculptor of all the figures on City Hall. His name was Alexander Milne Calder.)

At the unveiling on Thanksgiving Day, 1923, Leopold Stokowski led the Police Band and thousands of citizens in singing "The Star-Spangled Banner." Letters were read from Presidents Harding and Coolidge praising the successful businessman who had also served as Postmaster General, president of the YMCA and an active religious leader.

In the foundation of the monument is a box containing James Whitcomb Riley's poem "The Inner Side of Every Crowd," also a white aster, a letter from President Harding and a photograph of Mayor J. Hampton Moore, who was chairman of the committee to erect the statue.

While some monuments are neglected after installation, this statue was erected across the street from the Wanamaker store, which was committed to its care. A fund for perpetual maintenance was established to include twice-yearly oiling and regular polishing. In addition, a wreath was to be placed on it each year on Mr. Wanamaker's birthday.

6 *We turn the corner of City Hall and find*
John Christian Bullitt, whose descendant, William
Christian Bullitt, was the first U.S. ambassador to
the Soviet Union.

Bronze
Height: 9'10"
Base: granite (5'1")

North Plaza, City Hall
Installed 1907
Moved to present location 1936

John Christian Bullitt

JOHN J. BOYLE

John Christian Bullitt came to Philadelphia at the age of 25 from his native Kentucky and lived here for the rest of his life. As a lawyer he was so successful that he became a leader of the Bar. Bullitt's astute management of the financial house of Jay Cooke and Company during the panic of 1873 made his name famous. In 1884 he erected the first modern office building in Philadelphia at Fourth and Walnut Streets and was one of the founders of the Fourth Street National Bank, which quartered itself in the Bullitt Building.

Bullitt was one of the early advocates for what is now the Benjamin Franklin Parkway, and he was a delegate to the Pennsylvania State Constitutional Convention in 1873. But his chief claim to fame in Philadelphia was the "Bullitt Bill," which gave the city a new charter when it was passed in 1885. It reduced the number of city departments from 28 to 8 and placed them under the direct supervision of the mayor, who was given the power to appoint the department directors. The effect of this charter was to lodge real power with the mayor by abolishing all the commissions.

When he died in 1902, Bullitt's many admirers funded this commemorative statue.

7 *Guarding City Hall we see General John Fulton Reynolds, whose saber is stolen from time to time.*

Bronze
Height: 12′
Base: granite (10′)

North Plaza, City Hall
Dedicated 1884

General John Fulton Reynolds

JOHN ROGERS

General Reynolds was six feet tall and a superb horseman, inspiring to his troops. His fellow officers considered him a military genius and came to him for advice. At Gettysburg there is a monument to him on the spot where he was killed on the first day of that battle, July 1, 1863.

This is Philadelphia's first equestrian statue and first public monument to a Civil War soldier. A businessman, Joseph E. Temple, offered $25,000 toward the memorial. It was unveiled on Grand Army Day, September 18, 1884, and celebrated with a holiday and a parade of 10,000 people.

Three and a half tons of bronze went into the cast, and the sculptor, John Rogers, paid $15,000 for it. Rogers was known for his very popular parlor-sized "conversation groups," which consisted of small plaster figures depicting scenes from Shakespeare, life on the farm and Civil War episodes. During his lifetime he was said to have sold 100,000 copies.

General Reynolds was from Lancaster, Pennsylvania, where his father was publisher of the Lancaster *Journal* and a member of the state legislature. When the general died, never having married, he was survived by his three brothers, one of whom, William Reynolds, was a distinguished naval officer and explorer.

8 *The next figure we see is General George McClellan, who seems ready to ride across the traffic circle.*

Bronze
Height: 14½'
Base: black granite (10')

North Plaza, City Hall
Installed 1894

General George McClellan

HENRY JACKSON ELLICOT

When George McClellan returned from Europe, where he had been sent with a group of officers to study military systems, he proposed a new type of saddle. Modeled after the Hungarian saddle used by the Prussian cavalry, it became standard equipment for the U.S. Army and was known as the "McClellan saddle." Ironically, this equestrian statue, which was a gift to the city in 1894 from the Grand Army of the Republic, gets criticism from horsemen that the bridle and bits are improperly fitted.

McClellan, who was born in Philadelphia, was the son of the physician who founded Jefferson Medical College and was a descendant of a noble Scots family. When he went to West Point, he was an honor student and a classmate of Andrew Jackson. After his graduation, McClellan fought in the war with Mexico and worked as an engineer for the railroads until the outbreak of the Civil War. He was then given command of the Army of the Potomac and soon after was made commander-in-chief of all the northern armies.

When he turned back General Lee, McClellan became known as "The Hero of Antietam," but he waited so long to follow the retreating Confederates that Lee was able to regroup. This angered President Lincoln, and he relieved McClellan of his command and ordered him to report to Trenton, where he remained in retirement until 1864.

McClellan was well loved by his troops and when he was replaced, a Philadelphia admirer named Septimus Winner wrote a song called "Give Us Back Our Commander," which was a big hit but got Winner arrested for treason. When he was released from prison, Winner's father, a violin maker, gave him a fiddle made of floor boards taken from Independence Hall, and with this fiddle Winner composed the song "Listen to the Mockingbird."

Not many people know that McClellan ran against Lincoln in 1864 when the Democratic Party made him its presidential candidate. He was embarrassed by the party platform, which called for an end to the war, and he withdrew on election day. Lincoln won by 212 electoral votes to McClellan's 21, but in the popular vote, McClellan's total was only 400,000 less than Lincoln's.

In 1878, McClellan became governor of New Jersey, and by collecting and exhibiting European china, he inspired the Trenton pottery industry to enter into the manufacture of fine china. He was a disciple of the politics of involvement, believing, as he said to New Jerseyans in his inaugural address, "that it is the duty of each one of them to interest themselves in the affairs of his community as he does in his business."

9 *Standing back and considering all that has passed is Matthias Baldwin, whose statue was a gift to the city from the Baldwin Locomotive Works.*

Bronze
Height: 8′
Base: granite (10′8″)

North Plaza, City Hall
Unveiled 1906
Moved to present location 1921

Matthias William Baldwin

HERBERT ADAMS

When he was nine years old, Matthias Baldwin went to work as an apprentice jewelry maker for Woolworth Brothers of Philadelphia. Eventually he joined a firm that manufactured tools and engines. There he became interested in a new invention, the steam engine, and he founded the Baldwin Locomotive Works, where in 1832 he designed "Old Ironsides," a six-ton locomotive that still operates on a few feet of track at the Franklin Institute. "Old Ironsides," one of the first successful American models, was such a problem to assemble that when it was completed Baldwin remarked, "This is the last locomotive we'll ever build." But his company prospered and became the largest manufacturer of locomotives in the world.

Baldwin became a rich man, but his family life was not extravagant and he donated $10,000 a year to charities. In 1835, he founded a school for black children. He contributed to the Franklin Institute for the promotion of mechanical arts, and is also credited with helping to build seven churches in the city. "Wissinoming," his beautiful country estate, later became a home for the elderly.

Baldwin died in 1886 at the age of 91, and in 1906 his company erected his statue at Broad and Spring Garden Streets, where it overlooked his factory. In 1921, when that grassy spot was paved over, the sculpture was moved to City Hall. In one hand the statue holds a roll of blueprints; the other hand holds a tin horn. In 1974, Baldwin was inducted into the Pennsylvania Hall of Fame.

10

Now walk across to the corner of John F. Kennedy Boulevard and Broad Street. A very celebrated Philadelphian is honored here.

Bronze
Height: 10'
Base: granite

North Broad Street, opposite City Hall
Unveiled June 20, 1981

BENJAMIN FRANKLIN · CRAFTSMAN

Benjamin Franklin, Craftsman

JOSEPH BROWN

This sculpture of young Benjamin Franklin stands across from the Masonic Temple, whose members commissioned it in honor of the 250th anniversary of Free Masonry in Pennsylvania. There was a great deal of criticism in the news media about the esthetics of this piece when it was first unveiled, but no one mentioned that the sculptor had lost the sight of one eye and had failing vision in the other.

Joe Brown became a sculptor almost by accident. He was graduated from Temple University in 1931 at the height of the Depression. He couldn't get a position as a physical education instructor, but since he was an athlete he got a job posing for artists at the Pennsylvania Academy of the Fine Arts. There he was tempted to try sculpting himself, and the three pieces he produced were accepted by the Academy for exhibition. His work caught the eye of Dr. R. Tait McKenzie, a noted physician and sculptor. Brown served a seven-year apprenticeship to Dr. McKenzie and then joined the Princeton University staff as boxing coach in 1937. In 1939 he began teaching a sculpture course and eventually became a full professor in the School of Architecture.

Brown was a member of the Philadelphia Art Commission for 12 years, and Philadelphia has many of his bronze athletes in public places.

11

From the Franklin statue it is easy to see the Jacques Lipchitz monument, our next stop.

Bronze
Height: 33'
Base: polished granite

S.E. corner, Municipal Services Building Plaza
Dedicated April 27, 1976

Government of the People

JACQUES LIPCHITZ

Compared with the fanfare surrounding unveilings of monuments in our city's past, the dedication of this Lipchitz sculpture was quiet; only about 150 people attended. *Government of the People* is another controversial piece that has managed to survive its critics and join the public works as a familiar sight.

The story of this work is a recent one, so the details are well known. Six years after the city had commissioned it, the sculptor had produced a plaster model and had been paid $118,000 toward its total cost. The mayor of Philadelphia took exception to it and vowed that the city would not spend another cent on something that "looked like some plasterers had dropped a load of plaster." Other critics claimed that the work was "too abstract to be understood by the ordinary citizen." But the Fairmount Park Art Association raised $350,000, enough to have it cast in Italy, sent here and installed.

Government of the People is the last major piece of sculpture that Jacques Lipchitz produced before he died in 1973. At the dedication in 1976, his wife, Yulla, presented to the city the tools the artist had used to sculpt the work. This massive structure shows bodies of people interlocking to support one another and the flag of the city. Lipchitz thought of the composition as a modern totem pole. One art critic wrote that "*Government of the People* brings to a grand summation the familiar Lipchitz theme of salvation through courage, sacrifice and determination."

After all the years of controversy, the monument still evokes strong reactions, but the adjectives being used to describe it now include heroic, powerful and impressive. Its colossal proportions seem to belong in its space, and we have gotten accustomed to its excitement.

12

Sharing the plaza with the Lipchitz work is the sculpture portrait of Frank Rizzo.

Bronze
Height: 9'

Municipal Services Building Plaza
Installed 1999

Frank Rizzo (Mayor)

ZENOS FRUDAKIS

Frank Rizzo had a colorful and controversial career as police commissioner and then two-term mayor of Philadelphia (1972–80). He was a folk hero to many citizens, having risen from modest beginnings in the storied neighborhood of South Philadelphia. In 1991, he again ran for mayor and won a three-way primary election but died before the November election was held. At his viewing at the Cathedral of SS. Peter and Paul, thousands of people lined up day into night to pay their respects to the larger-than-life politician.

Then his friends proposed a collection of funds for a statue of Rizzo and the arguments began as to its eventual location. There were cartoons in the newspapers, public opinion articles, Art Commission suggestions and his family's approval to arbitrate. The monument by Jacques Lipchitz called *Government of the People,* which Rizzo had disliked when he was mayor, was in front of the Municipal Services Building, so that site was considered inappropriate for Rizzo's statue. However, his son, Councilman Frank Rizzo Jr., said that his father had mellowed since its installation and through the years had grown fond of it. So it was agreed that the Municipal Services Building Plaza would be the site and the sculptor, Zenos Frudakis, designed a likeness of the former mayor as if he were walking down the steps of the building with his arm outstretched to his constituents.

Frudakis, a native of San Francisco, has been in Philadelphia since he attended the Pennsylvania Academy of the Fine Arts on scholarship. He then went on to earn a B.F.A. and an M.F.A. at the University of Pennsylvania. He is a well-known teacher as well as a sculptor of celebrities. His bronze relief of another former mayor of Philadelphia, Richardson Dilworth, is located in the Philadelphia Airport's International Terminal, which is named for him. Frudakis has also had commissions to do sculptures of children, birds and animals. The Philadelphia Zoo has his life-sized jaguars. He works all the time and even designed a traveling box for clay to take on long airplane trips in order to make that time productive.

13

*Continue to 15th Street and Kennedy Plaza.
Near the fountain, a favorite noontime spot
for Center City workers, we find LOVE.*

Painted aluminum
Height: 6′
Base: stainless steel (7′)

Kennedy Plaza
Installed 1978

Philadelphia LOVE

ROBERT INDIANA

In 1976, Robert Indiana (whose real name is Robert Clark) had his agency arrange to loan this sculpture to Philadelphia for the Bicentennial, and for two years it stood on its pedestal while negotiations for its purchase were unsuccessful. Finally, when the city officials refused the price of $45,000, the agency's gallery came by one day and quietly repossessed it. Widespread public dismay caused the city to try to buy it back. In an *Inquirer* editorial the loss of the sculpture was called "a casualty of appalling City Hall insensitivity to esthetic value." F. Eugene Dixon Jr., a businessman, sportsman and chairman of the Philadelphia Art Commission, offered to pay for it and Philadelphia got it back.

Indiana, on a tour, confessed to a group of students at the Philadelphia College of Art that he was "not a sculptor by any means. It was one of my worst subjects at school.

I don't have any feeling for it at all." But he has been obsessed with word images, giving them three-dimensional shape. Indiana worked on the "love" theme for many years, experimenting with foreign languages including Hebrew and Chinese. *LOVE* is a tribute not only to his formal precision, but to his faith in the power of what must be the most abused word in modern usage. He feels that the tilted "O" makes his composition more dynamic. It's been called the most plagiarized piece of artwork in the country. In 1968, two women entrepreneurs marketed a gold ring featuring Indiana's "LOVE" motif. It has appeared on popular posters and even U.S. postage stamps.

In 1978 the *Philadelphia Inquirer* quoted Indiana's conclusion that "Love is the biggest subject in the whole world."

14 *Now we leave Kennedy Plaza, cross over Arch Street and begin our course on the handsome Benjamin Franklin Parkway.*

The Benjamin Franklin Parkway

In the 1880s it took foresight to imagine a highway from the city to the park. The way was filled with buildings of every sort, but in 1884 a proposal was made that "a convenient approach to the park is a necessity. Why not make it something worthy of the magnificent City of Philadelphia?" Wheels grind slowly and it wasn't until 1891 that a petition was drawn and the project endorsed. There was immediate opposition; people complained that the city planners were trying to be too fancy and were imitating nobility at the expense of ordinary folk. They were afraid that only the rich could afford the carriages to ride down such a street. For a while the enterprise seemed dead. Then, in 1904, City Hall was completed and the idea was revived in order to have a dramatic gateway to the park.

In 1907 the Fairmount Park Art Association brought in experts. The architectural firm of Cret, Trumbauer and Zantzinger presented a plan that incorporated the ideas of Jacques Greber. Greber, a famous French city planner and architect, based his design for the parkway on the Champs Élysées of Paris. It required condemning whole blocks of properties. In 1915 the people of Philadelphia voted nine million dollars for the project, but the costs eventually totaled more than twice as much. The task was accomplished by the devotion of citizens like Eli Kirk Price Jr. and Congressman James Beck, who fought the obstructionists, cajoled the unconvinced and dealt with the stubborn, unglamorous day-to-day details until it was completed. In 1918 the Benjamin Franklin Parkway was opened to traffic, and then the new struggle began: the building of the Art Museum as its crowning jewel. Work on the museum was begun in 1920 and it opened in 1928 at a cost of more than twelve million dollars.

Today we have a beautiful boulevard decorated with the flags of all nations and extending from City Hall at one end to our own imposing Parthenon at the other. And now we can do what James Beck, who fought so long and hard for the Parkway, could only dream of doing in 1921, on the 50th anniversary of the Fairmount Park Art Association: "I would like to come back a hundred years from now and walk up the Parkway and climb at last the flight of steps that will lead to the central temple of the Art Gallery and look over Philadelphia."

15 *We now proceed to 16th Street and the Parkway. Here* The Prophet *stands patiently, stroking his beard.*

Marble
Height: 8′
Weight: 9,000 lbs.
Base: stone

16th Street and Benjamin Franklin Parkway
Installed 1974

The Prophet

JACOB LIPKIN

Jacob Lipkin frequently won medals in New Jersey's annual exhibitions of the Painters' and Sculptors' Society. He is a stone and wood carver of such large compositions that when Provident National Bank gave him a one-man show, *The Prophet* could not fit into the space reserved for it. It was placed temporarily outside of the Hospitality Center where, a newspaper reported, "it was generally ignored."

In 1974, however, it was given a permanent site. There was no fanfare. One morning some workmen, using a crane to lift it, trucked it over to a hastily made base and set it down.

16

Proceeding a little farther on the Parkway, we come to the Henry Moore sculpture that was moved to this location in 1990.

Bronze
Height: 4½′
Base: granite

17th Street and Benjamin Franklin Parkway
Unveiled 1967

Three-Way Piece Number 1: Points

HENRY MOORE

Henry Moore once said, "The observation of nature is part of an artist's life. . . ." But he wished that "sculpture should always at first sight have some obscurities, and further meanings." This massive work, perched on three points, certainly fulfills his wish. In a 1934 essay, Moore expressed his belief that "a work can have in it a pent-up energy, an intense life of its own, independent of the object it may represent."

Moore finished this piece in 1964, and it was bought in 1967 by the Fairmount Park Art Association. This world-famous English artist made many works in wood, stone and cement without first using clay models. Often they have organic shapes, and it is characteristic of them to have holes as part of the composition. "Beauty," he said, "in the Greek or Renaissance sense, is not the aim of my sculpture." His intention was not to decorate but to express the essence of life and stimulate excitement in it.

During the air raids on London in World War II, the sight of hundreds of people huddling in the subways inspired Moore to create a famous series of drawings, the "Shelter Sketches." These showed people under blankets lying patiently in "a timeless expression of human endurance." The association of human figures with landscape forms is a recurring theme in his works.

17

We now pass the former Pennwalt Building, Friends Select School and the United Way building to reach Kopernik *on the Torun Triangle. Across the Parkway stands the statue of another great Polish hero, General Kosciuszko, but he's on our return trip.*

Stainless steel superstructure
Height: 12′
Base: granite (12′)

Benjamin Franklin Parkway at 18th Street
Dedicated August 18, 1973

Kopernik

DUDLEY TALCOTT

Mikolaj Kopernik (1473–1543), generally known by his Latin name Nicolaus Copernicus, was the Polish astronomer who discovered that the earth revolved around the sun. His theory was expounded in his life's work, *Concerning the Revolution of the Celestial Spheres,* and he received the first printed copy of it as he lay on his deathbed. His concept was later corroborated by the German astronomer Johannes Kepler, and formed the basis for the law of gravity discovered by the English scientist Sir Isaac Newton.

The Polish Heritage Society of Philadelphia first proposed the idea for a Kopernik monument and initiated a steering committee. After a nationwide search for an artist, Dudley Talcott of Farmingdale, Connecticut, was selected. His idea was an abstract depiction of Kopernik's heliocentric system: a stainless steel ring, sixteen feet in diameter, symbolizing the orbit of the earth, and a sun in the center with rays extending out into infinity. The orbit of the earth and the sun disk are supported on a stainless steel angle that symbolizes the homemade instruments used by Kopernik for his calculations.

The Philadelphia Art Commission immediately approved Talcott's model, and Polish-Americans together with the American Council of Polish Clubs raised $60,000 to finance this gift to Philadelphia. The dedication, on the 500th anniversary of Kopernik's birth, was the highlight of a year-long celebration of Polish-American heritage, and the monument was installed with great ceremony at a choice site on the Parkway.

In 1976 the town of Torun, Poland, the birthplace of Copernicus, was officially designated as a sister city to Philadelphia, and the triangular plot on which the Kopernik monument is located was named the Torun Triangle.

18

*Across Race Street, in the corner garden of
the Cathedral of SS. Peter and Paul, is
Walter Erlebacher's Jesus Breaking Bread.
One art critic was pleased that the
sculpture stands almost at ground level.
"It is meant to be an accessible Jesus,"
he remarked, "not a Jesus on a pedestal."*

Bronze
Height: 6′
Base: marble (4′)

18th Street and Benjamin Franklin Parkway
Dedicated May 1978

Jesus Breaking Bread

WALTER ERLEBACHER

This sculpture portrays Jesus holding a piece of broken bread in each hand. The bread symbolizes Christ as the spiritual food received in the Holy Communion. The figure is flanked by wheat sheaves and grape clusters, which symbolize the Eucharistic elements of bread and wine.

The work was commissioned for the International Eucharistic Congress, which attracted more than a million visitors to Philadelphia in 1976. The theme of the Congress was "The Hunger of the Human Family." During the meeting of the Congress, the statue was on exhibit at the Civic Center.

Walter Erlebacher was a teacher at the Philadelphia College of Art, and his style has been called "unconventional realism." Some of his best-known works include *The Death of Apollo* and *Night and Day Teaching Their Son to Walk*.

19

Now our course turns up 18th Street for a half block. We cross over to a grassy section occupied by a statue of Thomas Fitzsimons by Giuseppe Donato, who also did the frieze on the west pediment of the Municipal Court Building on Vine Street.

Bronze
Height: 8′
Base: granite (6′7″)

18th Street opposite SS. Peter and Paul
Installed September 16, 1946

Thomas Fitzsimons

GIUSEPPE DONATO

Thomas Fitzsimons was the only one of the 38 signers of the Constitution whose portrait is missing. Historians searched for a picture of him for years without success. In 1937 an artist, Herman Klein, was sent to interview the colonial leader's descendants. He painted a picture from the impression he formed while reading old records and family legends. In 1940 the Society of the Friendly Sons of St. Patrick approved a proposal for a monument in honor of Fitzsimons, who was one of the society's original members. With the Klein painting as his only guide, the Philadelphia sculptor Giuseppe Donato designed a statue that was finished in 1941 but was not cast in bronze until after World War II was over. It was finally installed and dedicated in 1946.

Fitzsimons has a rags-to-riches story. He was born in Ireland and came here young and poor, but he established himself in business and became one of Philadelphia's leading activists. He supported the colonists against England and fought in the Revolutionary War in a company he himself had formed. Toward the end of the war he lobbied hard to induce the government to pay all that was owed to the soldiers before they were demobilized.

Later Fitzsimons was elected to the Continental Congress and was a member of the Convention that framed the Constitution of 1787. He led the parade that celebrated its ratification on July 4, 1788. For many years Fitzsimons was the president of the Philadelphia Chamber of Commerce and he won wide respect among colonial businessmen for his high morals and philanthropy. He was the founder and director of the Bank of North America, director and then president of the Insurance Company of North America, trustee of the University of Pennsylvania and a member of the Hibernian Society and the Hibernia Fire Company. In addition, he served six years in the first national House of Representatives.

Fitzsimons survived a bankruptcy but never recouped his former prestige. He died at the age of 70 in 1811 and is buried in Old St. Mary's Catholic Church at Fourth and Spruce Streets.

20

Next to Fitzsimons is the statue of an eighteenth-century diplomat given to the city by the king of Spain.

Bronze
Height: 15′
Base: pink granite

18th Street opposite SS. Peter and Paul
Installed 1977

Diego de Gardoqui

ANTONIO SANGUIN

In 1977, Juan Carlos I presented this work to Philadelphia in commemoration of the Bicentennial. The sculptor was Antonio Sanguin, who was Spanish-born but moved to the United States.

Don Diego de Gardoqui had a big job in the New World. He was the envoy of the king of Spain at the time of the American Revolution. Spain was in control of the Louisiana territory, as well as Florida, Cuba and Puerto Rico, and Don Diego's office handled the passport business to Spanish America and the communications between the governments. Spain supported the colonies against England, and Don Diego brought contributions of money and 30,000 blankets to the Revolutionary Army.

In his diary, George Washington mentioned several evenings spent in the company of Don Diego, who came from New York to Philadelphia especially to see him.

21

Turning to the left, we walk a few steps to a figure in a chariot flanked by lions. It seems a curious way to depict a hero with a Quaker upbringing.

Bronze
Height: 10′8″
Base: limestone (8′10″)

Municipal Court Building, north of 18th Street
Installed 1934

General Galusha Pennypacker

ALBERT LAESSLE

During the Civil War, the handsome 22-year-old Galusha Pennypacker was the youngest brigadier general in either the Union or Confederate forces. This memorial symbolizes his fearlessness when in the face of certain death, he seized the flag and led his brigade to victory. For that heroism at Fort Fisher, North Carolina, Congress voted him the Congressional Medal of Honor. He was seriously wounded in that action, however, and the wound never healed. For the rest of his life he suffered intense pain without complaint and fulfilled an active military career. He was wounded in action fourteen times.

The peacetime service of General Pennypacker was equally outstanding. He was commander of various posts in the South during Reconstruction, and his kindness, courtesy, tact and patience won the respect and affection of the Southern people, doing much to reconcile them to the federal government.

Albert Laessle took over the execution of this work from Charles Grafly, whose health had failed. Laessle had won many prizes for lifelike animal sculptures. In fact, when the sculptor was 24, he exhibited a group called *Turtle and Lizards,* which was so realistic that he was accused of casting it directly from life. To repudiate the charge, he modeled another turtle in wax. After that he often used the turtle shell, with his name on it, somewhere in his works. There are thirteen scales on a turtle shell and thirteen letters in his name, which is another reason Laessle used the shell as his logo.

22

Continuing past Pennypacker to the sidewalk on the Parkway, we walk along until we reach the Shakespeare Memorial, which is opposite the Free Library.

Bronze
Height: 6′
Base: Pennsylvania marble (14′2″)

Benjamin Franklin Parkway opposite
the Free Library
Dedicated October 1928

Shakespeare Memorial

ALEXANDER STIRLING CALDER

On top of tall shafts of black Pennsylvania marble sit two bronze figures. One is a representation of Tragedy as Hamlet, the melancholy Dane, and the other, Comedy, is symbolized in the figure of Touchstone, the fool.

On the front of the base are the familiar words from Shakespeare's *As You Like It:* "All the world's a stage and all the men and women merely players."

This work is considered to be one of Alexander Stirling Calder's masterpieces and one of the finest memorials to Shakespeare in the United States. In 1928 a newspaper wrote that "for generations to come Mr. Calder's genius, as represented in this sculpture, will be a source of unfailing inspiration."

On the back of the pedestal, facing the Free Library, are the names of ten famous actors, "who brought lustre to the Philadelphia stage." On a third side of the base is a tribute to four Shakespearean scholars who "added to the distinction of Philadelphia letters."

The monument, erected in 1928 by the Shakspere Society and the Fairmount Park Art Association, reflects the controversy over the correct spelling of Shakespeare's name. It is spelled two ways on the shaft—the commonly accepted way and the way the Bard supposedly spelled it when he last wrote his name, "Shakspere."

23

We now proceed in the same direction to the white pylons of the Civil War Memorial.

Tennessee marble
Height: 52'
Bases: granite

Benjamin Franklin Parkway
above 20th Street
Installed 1921

Civil War Soldiers and Sailors Memorial

HERMON ATKINS MACNEIL

In 1918, in a burst of patriotism, the City of Philadelphia appropriated $88,000 for a Civil War memorial. This monument, designed to honor soldiers, sailors and marines, involved the efforts of a sculptor, an architect and several stone carvers. The figures on the pylon to the left are dedicated to soldiers and those on the right to sailors.

In 1956 the shafts were moved 150 feet to their present locations, at a cost of $30,000, in order to make room for the underpass of the Vine Street Expressway. They are positioned as a gateway to the Art Museum at one end of the Parkway.

As a young artist, Hermon MacNeil had become fascinated with the subject of American Indians. To him "they were as fine as Greek warriors and as worthy to be immortalized." But after he got involved in his commissions for war memorials, military themes took the place of his earlier absorption with the Native Americans. MacNeil was also a designer of United States quarter-dollars and the Pan American Medal.

24

Our tour continues on the north side of the Parkway. On our right are two groups of figures.

Bronze
Height: 12′
Length: 20′
Width: 5′

20th Street and Benjamin Franklin Parkway, outside the Youth Study Center
Unveiled November 1956

The Spirit of Juveniles: The Great Mother/The Great Doctor

WALDEMAR RAEMISCH

Two of the members of the Philadelphia Art Commission strongly objected to this work when it was first presented. One called the figures "pie-faced" but then reversed his "No" vote and agreed to the project.

These two groups of statues stand outside of the Youth Study Center, where troubled juveniles are kept temporarily. The figures are twice life-sized and are specially adapted to be seen from the street. Up close, they are not so graceful. The group on the right (as one faces them) conveys the theme of "The Great Mother" and the one on the left that of "The Great Doctor."

When sculptor Waldemar Raemisch was a 14-year-old boy in Germany, he was apprenticed to a metalsmith, and eventually he became a prominent artist. He came to America as a refugee in 1939, and by 1946 he had become chairman of the Sculpture Department at the Rhode Island School of Design.

Raemisch spent two and a half years on this project, but he died suddenly while supervising the casting in Rome. The National Gold Medal Exhibition of the Architectural League of New York, which usually gives gold medals only to living sculptors, gave him a special citation for this work.

25

We now proceed one city block further to the front of the Rodin Museum. This museum was the dream of Jules Mastbaum, who died before it could be built. Thousands of people came to his funeral, and the French ambassador presented his widow with the Cross of the Chevalier Legion of Honor. Jacques Greber, the architect who had laid out the Parkway, designed this building, which houses the largest collection of Rodin sculptures outside of France.

Bronze
Height: 6′7″
Base: limestone

Rodin Museum, Benjamin Franklin Parkway at 22nd Street
Installed November 20, 1929

The Thinker

AUGUSTE RODIN

Rodin was the son of a police inspector who reportedly said, "Artists are idlers and good-for-nothings." Rodin himself feuded with the art establishment most of his life, and it was not until he was 63 that the French government conferred on him the rank of Commander in the Legion of Honor.

Rodin's early sculpture was so realistic that when he exhibited his *Age of Bronze,* he was accused of having made his casts directly from the human figure. This infuriated the sculptor, who was determined to prove that he had no need to employ cheap tricks. He produced a profusion of figures in low relief and in small scale for the *Gates of Hell,* which was inspired by the *Divine Comedy.* One of the small figures represents the poet Dante contemplating his "Inferno" and can be seen at the entrance to the Rodin Museum. Concerning *The Thinker*, installed outside the museum, Rodin reportedly wrote to an art critic: "Guided by my first inspiration, I conceived another thinker, a naked man, his fist against his teeth, he dreams. The fertile thought slowly elaborated itself within his brain. He is no longer dreamer, he is creator."

He is also quoted as saying, "What makes my 'Thinker' think is that he thinks not only with his brain, with his knotted brow, his distended nostrils, compressed lips, but with every muscle of his arms, back and legs, with his clenched fists and gripping toes."

Rodin lived to see *The Thinker* become the worldwide symbol of the artist.

26 *Crossing to the center and continuing up the Parkway, we come to the Eakins Oval. In the distance is Philadelphia's* Washington Monument. *Flanked by twin fountains, the monument is a favorite with visitors who climb on it to pose for pictures and to read the names on the reliefs. It was reported that the German sculptor Rudolph Siemering had originally designed the central figure as Frederick the Great. When he got the American commission, he used the same casting and simply changed the hat and the medals.*

Bronze and granite
Height: 44′

Benjamin Franklin Parkway opposite the Philadelphia Museum of Art
Unveiled 1897

The Washington Monument

RUDOLPH SIEMERING

Great crowds converged on Fairmount Park to see President McKinley unveil the colossal bronze equestrian statue of George Washington. The festivities were held at the original site, the Green Street entrance to the park, and it is said that the work cost more than $250,000, an enormous expenditure at that time.

Several steamers were operating on the Schuylkill River that day. An extra one, pressed into service to handle the crowds, was a small one-deck launch that went out of control and was swept over the dam. Three of the fifteen people aboard her drowned.

The movement to build a monument to Washington began as early as 1810, but the War of 1812 intervened and in 1824, when Lafayette visited Philadelphia, there was a great deal of embarrassment because the city fathers could not show him a single memorial to the great general.

At long last the Society of Cincinnati of Pennsylvania, an organization made up of descendants of officers who had served under Washington, gave the contract for a monument to a well-known German sculptor, Rudolph Siemering. He was dedicated to accurate and realistic portrayals of Revolutionary War heroes and American symbols, and he tried to say everything in one huge composition.

Washington is shown on horseback, dressed in the uniform of the Revolutionary Army, atop a high granite pedestal. The pedestal is in the center of four fountains, which symbolize four American rivers: the Delaware, the Potomac, the Hudson and the Mississippi. Guarding each river are typical American animals such as buffalo, elk and moose. The thirteen steps of the base represent the original thirteen states, and they lead up to the pedestal on all four sides.

On the front of the pedestal is a group symbolizing America receiving trophies from her victorious sons. On the back of the pedestal is another group showing America arousing her sons to the dangers of slavery. The other two sides of the pedestal are decorated with bronze low reliefs, one representing the march of the American army and the other commemorating the westward movement of the American people. Many names of historical significance are cut into the panels.

In 1926, when the Parkway was ready for it, the monument was moved to its present site at a cost of $80,000.

27

Proceeding on to the fountains, we find that the first bears an inscription that runs entirely around its basin: "Dedicated to the memory of Captain John Ericsson, Scientist, Inventor, Patriot, born in Sweden, died in America, the country of his adoption."

Marble

Benjamin Franklin Parkway, Eakins Oval

Captain John Ericsson Fountain

HORACE TRUMBAUER, CHARLES E. BORIE JR. AND ALFRED ZANTZINGER

John Ericsson was a direct descendant of Leif Ericson, believed by many to be the Norse discoverer of America. His ancestor would have been proud of his achievements.

Ericsson was an inventor and engineer with a long list of patents and honors from all over the world. Although he was born in Sweden, he lived in the United States for fifty years and became an American hero. His iron-clad *Monitor* fought and won a famous naval battle with the larger Confederate *Merrimac* and helped to turn the tide of the Civil War. Ericsson also invented the caloric engine and the screw propeller, and developed ships with submarine cannon. Always searching for a new source of motive power, he experimented with an appliance to get mechanical energy from the sun, a "sun-motor."

When he died, Ericsson's body was escorted by a Navy cruiser from New York to Stockholm, Sweden.

Horace Trumbauer was an incredibly successful and prolific architect. In his long career he and his office of designers turned out over 400 country houses, townhouses and public buildings all over the country. Among his commissions were Duke University, the Philadelphia Museum of Art, the Philadelphia Free Library, Jefferson Medical College, the Ritz-Carlton and Benjamin Franklin hotels, Philmont Country Club and the Racquet Club. After his death, Trumbauer's lovely home in Wynnefield was kept open for public tours.

28

The Ericsson Fountain has a twin,
differing only in its inscription:
"In memory of Eli Kirk Price (1860–1933)
whose wisdom and dedication were
responsible for the development of the
Parkway and the Museum."

Marble

Benjamin Franklin Parkway, Eakins Oval

Eli Kirk Price Jr. Fountain

HORACE TRUMBAUER, CHARLES E. BORIE JR. AND ALFRED ZANTZINGER

Eli Kirk Price Jr. always asked himself the question, "Am I right?" If he believed he was, nothing would deter him from his chosen projects. Price was a lawyer in a distinguished family firm, but he regarded the development of the Benjamin Franklin Parkway and the Philadelphia Museum of Art as his life's work. He withstood storms of abuse and ridicule for his efforts.

The Price family has a long history of service in this city. Price's grandfather ran for the state senate in order to be in a position to secure passage of the Consolidation Act. This was a charter that is believed to have laid the foundation for Philadelphia's growth and importance. He was also one of the founders of Fairmount Park. Price's son, Philip, continued the family's involvement by serving as president of the Fairmount Park Art Association and vice president of the Fairmount Park Commission.

It was Eli Price's suggestion that the old waterworks be moved from the acropolis known as Faire Mount in order to provide a site for an art museum. It was under his presidency of the Fairmount Park Art Association in 1925 that construction of the Philadelphia Museum of Art was completed. Price received many awards and honors for a lifetime of efforts to bring beauty to this city.

29

Crossing the street to the Art Museum side, we now follow the sidewalk to the right and encounter the Charioteer of Delphi. *The original of this figure was commissioned by Polyzalus, the Tyrant of Gela in Sicily, about 478 B.C. It was dedicated to Apollo as a token of thanks for a victory in a chariot race. The Greek sculptors Nikos Kerlis and Theodora Papayannis created this replica in faithful detail, including the inlaid eyes of the original.*

Bronze
Height: 4′
Base: marble (2′3″)

East Grounds, Philadelphia Museum of Art
Unveiled July 4, 1977

Charioteer of Delphi

Philadelphia was the recipient of several statues in honor of the American Bicentennial. The Greek government sent this gift as a symbol of Greek culture from the "cradle of democracy in the old world to the cradle of democracy in the new world."

This figure is the only authorized copy of the fifth century B.C. original, housed in the museum at Delphi. It represents the winning driver of a chariot race held at the Pythian games. These games were held every four years in ancient Delphi (one year before each Olympiad), and they included musical, literary and athletic contests.

Art critics complained that the location of the *Charioteer* does not show it to advantage.

30

Continuing on we come to the dazzling golden girl astride her horse with banner held on high.

Gilded bronze
Height: 15′
Base: granite (8′4″)

Kelly Drive opposite the Philadelphia Museum of Art
Dedicated 1890
Moved to present location 1948

Joan of Arc

EMMANUEL FRÉMIET

The sculptor, Emmanuel Frémiet, had made a contract that only three editions of his *Joan of Arc* would be cast, and three exist today: one in the Place des Pyramides, Paris; one in Nancy, France; and one in Philadelphia. But in 1905 he made some minor variations to keep to the letter of the contract and produced a *Joan of Arc* for the National Gallery of Victoria, Australia.

Because of a strange maneuver we have the original statue cast by Frémiet for Paris. It was a great success in 1874 when it was installed in the Place des Pyramides, but its creator was not satisfied with it and made another almost exactly like it. He asked the French authorities for permission to substitute the new one for the first, but they refused his request.

In 1890, when the Fairmount Park Art Association contracted to buy the newer version, Frémiet borrowed the original from Paris, saying that he wanted to gild it so that it would stand out in the midst of the dark buildings that surrounded it. Instead he gilded the newer one and returned it to the French authorities, and we in Philadelphia were given the ungilded original. This artistic hoax was not discovered until many years later.

In the meantime our Joan of Arc was moved from the east end of Girard Avenue Bridge, where it had stood since 1890. It was felt that the work was not fully appreciated at the old location, and in 1948 it was moved closer to Center City. In 1959 it was moved to the basement of the Art Museum to be gilded.

There is a tragic coincidence to add to the story of this remarkable statue. St. Joan of Arc was born in 1412 and was burned at the stake by the English in 1431 after she was captured in battle during the Hundred Years War. The model for this statue, Valerie Laneau, was a 15-year-old country girl who came to Paris and caught the eye of the sculptor because of her fine features. Sixty-two years later, Laneau, still in Paris, came home one night, lit her evening lamp and it exploded. She was burned to death.

31

Across the street from our Joan is a statue commemorating a martyrdom of a different kind.

Bronze
Height: 22'
Base: red granite

Kelly Drive
Unveiled April 24, 1976

Meher

KHOREN DER HAROOTIAN

The Armenians, in 301 A.D., were the first nation to declare Christianity their state religion. They kept their faith alive through centuries of fighting off the Persians, the Arabs and the Turks. Despite persecutions and invasions they established a civilized, family-oriented society with a tradition of education and business. But in 1915 a Turkish plan for their destruction culminated in the massacre of millions of their people. Those who could escaped to other parts of the world. The Armenian community in Philadelphia formed a committee to commemorate April 24, 1915, the "Day of Infamy," and also to commemorate the bicentennial of American independence. They collected $100,000 for this memorial as a symbol of the martyrdom of the Armenian nation and their gratitude for freedom in their adopted country.

The sculptor they chose, Khoren Der Harootian, spent much of his childhood hiding from Turkish invaders. His father, who was a priest, was killed in 1915. In 1921, Harootian was able to come to the United States, where he started his career as a painter. He saw this work as a triumph of the spirit of man. Meher is a powerful legendary figure of the Middle Ages, symbolizing the invincible faith of the Armenian people. On the statue's base are relief panels depicting their historic struggles and triumphs.

In 1950, Harootian was commissioned to sculpt a nine-foot-high granite figure, *The Scientist*, for the Ellen Phillips Samuel Memorial in Fairmount Park. In 1954 he won the gold medal of the Pennsylvania Academy of the Fine Arts.

32

Now we climb up the curving road to the west terrace of the Art Museum. On our right stands General Peter Muhlenberg.

Bronze
Height: 9′
Base: granite

Philadelphia Museum of Art, West Plaza Drive
Unveiled October 6, 1910

Major General Peter Muhlenberg

J. OTTO SCHWEIG

At City Hall, on October 6, 1910, the German-American citizens of Philadelphia staged the most elaborate demonstration they had ever undertaken. It was a celebration of the unveiling of a statue honoring General Peter Muhlenberg. At the outbreak of the Revolution, this Lutheran minister spoke his mind: "There was a time for all things, a time to preach and a time to fight. Now is the time to fight." After the war he became a member of Congress and then a United States senator from Pennsylvania. His father, Henry, was the revered founder and patriarch of the Lutheran Church in America.

This sculpture, commissioned by the German Society of Pennsylvania, shows Muhlenberg dressed in the uniform of a Continental Army officer but holding his clerical cloak on his arm. The front side of the pedestal shows a scene in low relief of the Lutheran Church in Woodstock, Virginia, of which he was pastor; another side shows battles in which he participated; the third side shows the positions he held; and the fourth side bears the seal of the German Society of which he was president in 1788, 1802 and 1807.

In 1928 the statues of Muhlenberg and Stephen Girard were moved from City Hall to Reyburn Plaza (now Municipal Services Building Plaza) because of the building of subway entrances. Then they were moved again for the construction of the Municipal Services Building. Now they face each other at the head of the Reiley Memorial sculpture terrace. In 1951, some Muhlenberg College freshmen took one look at the general's statue and volunteered to scrub it with soap and water.

33

Facing the general from across the terrace is Stephen Girard.

Bronze
Height: 9′3″
Base: granite (9′1″)

Philadelphia Museum of Art, West Plaza
Originally unveiled May 20, 1897

Stephen Girard

JOHN MASSEY RHIND

How many of us know that Stephen Girard saved our country from financial disaster? During the War of 1812, the federal Treasury was on the verge of bankruptcy and unable to borrow funds. Girard and his bank marketed sixteen million dollars' worth of bonds for the floundering government, which bolstered its credit and enabled the country to bring the war to a successful close. At that time Stephen Girard and John Jacob Astor were the two richest men in the United States. Girard's banking career, combined with his great shipping business, had made him the first millionaire merchant in the country. People were constantly appealing to him for funds. In 1822, even the president, James Monroe, asked Girard to lend him some money, saying that public service had made him neglect his private affairs.

What an amazing man Girard was. He overcame tragedies and failures to become "one of the great benefactors of mankind." He was born in France, and when he was 8 years old, he lost his right eye in an accident. Then when he was 12, his mother died and his father, left with ten children to rear, married a woman with ten children of her own. This made for a very crowded household, so at the age of 14, Girard went off to sea as a cabin boy and eventually became a licensed ship officer.

In 1776, he was on a trading ship when it was blockaded by the British at the entrance to Delaware Bay, and he escaped by sailing to Philadelphia. Here he opened a store, married a pretty girl ten years younger than himself, and cast his lot with the city. Sadly, after eight years of marriage, his wife, Mary, became mentally ill and he found it necessary to place her in the care of Pennsylvania Hospital. She lived there comfortably until her death 25 years later. For her long care, Girard left the hospital $30,000 in his will.

Girard left tremendous sums for public benefits. His most famous bequest provided land and money to build and maintain a residential school for fatherless boys. He stipulated that the boys were to be between 6 and 10 years old and were to stay until they were 18. They were to be given a sound education, food and clothes, and taught to be moral people. Girard College has had more than 18,000 graduates, and now girls are also admitted.

On the fiftieth anniversary of the opening of Girard College, its alumni and sponsors presented the city with this statue of Girard in loving tribute to his memory. Twenty-five sculptors had submitted models, and the art committee selected one by the noted sculptor John Massey Rhind. Girard stands in a comfortable position holding his glasses and wearing fashionable clothes. It was originally placed on Reyburn Plaza (now Municipal Services Building Plaza) but was moved to the Art Museum when the Municipal Services Building was being constructed. Inside the figure are two hermetically sealed cylinders that contain a copy of Girard's will, newspapers of the day and documents concerning Girard College. Cut into the base of the monument is a low relief of Girard's famous trading ship, *Water-Witch*. On the sides are two bronze panels, one representing his career as "Mariner and Merchant," and the other exemplifying his generosity with a view of Girard College. On the back of the pedestal is the inscription "Philadelphia's Greatest Philanthropist."

Terrace of Heroes: Reilly Memorial

34

We can now take a look at the Terrace of Heroes *by descending the steps on the right-hand side. In 1968, protesters opposed to the military draft put gags on all six of the historic figures in this group. When no one seemed to notice their symbolic act, the young men ended up calling the police themselves to report it.*

Philadelphia Museum of Art, West Terrace

Brigadier General William Moffett Reilly served a lifetime in the Voluntary Militia and the Pennsylvania National Guard. When he died a bachelor in 1896, he left his estate in a trust fund to erect bronze memorials to Revolutionary War heroes. He singled out Lafayette, Montgomery, Pulaski and von Steuben because they were not born in this country: "Natives of France, Ireland, Poland and Germany, young, ardent and animated by intense love of liberty, renouncing every selfish and material interest, they threw themselves into the cause of emancipating the colonies from the yoke of the British tyranny. They were inspired by the nobler humanity which rises above the love of one's own country only—the love of liberty for all mankind without regard to race or creed. . . ."

By 1938 the trust fund had accumulated $112,000 over the original principal of $57,000, and by 1949 the statues were completed. General Reilly, however, had specified that the statues were to stand by that of George Washington in front of Independence Hall. After the art jury vetoed this plan in 1938, President Judge Van Dusen of Orphan's Court was asked to decide. He suggested the present location. In addition, Reilly's will stated that if funds permitted, other Revolutionary War heroes should be honored as well. In 1957, John Paul Jones was included in the *Terrace of Heroes*, as was Nathaniel Greene in 1962. Louis Borie, a Philadelphia architect, designed the bases.

From Reilly's will across the decades come these words: "I now make this provision for the erection of statues not only to commemorate their glorious deeds, but also as testimonials of appreciation and gratitude to the lands which gave these liberty-loving men their birth."

General Casimir Pulaski

SIDNEY WAUGH

Bronze
Height: 9′4″
Base: granite (7′6″)

Installed 1947

Born in Poland, Casimir Pulaski fought heroically with his father, Count Joseph Pulaski, to combat Russian domination of Poland, but they were defeated and their estate confiscated. Pulaski escaped to Turkey and then to Paris, hoping to get help for Poland. In Paris, he decided to join the colonies in the American Revolution. He came to Boston with a letter from Benjamin Franklin and met George Washington. In 1777, he was commissioned a brigadier general, and he served at Brandywine and Germantown. However, in 1778, he resigned a cavalry command rather than continue to serve under General Anthony Wayne. Soon he was given permission to organize his own cavalry unit, the Pulaski Legion, which fought gallantly. Sadly, in 1779, while leading the attack on Savannah, he was mortally wounded.

The federal government, in 1929, named Fort Pulaski, at the mouth of the Savannah River, after him. Cockspur Island, Georgia, is designated as the Fort Pulaski National Monument.

Admiral John Paul Jones

WALKER HANCOCK

Bronze
Height: 9′4″
Base: granite (7′8″)

Installed 1957

Born in Scotland, this future admiral went to sea when he was twelve. At the age of 24, he was placed in command of a ship. His crew mutinied and he killed one of the sailors in self-defense. To avoid trial he ran away, arriving in Philadelphia in 1775, having added the surname "Jones" to his real name, John Paul.

A friend got Jones a commission in the Continental Navy, and he became a daring hero of raids on the enemy. He captured the *Drake*, the first British warship to surrender to a Continental ship. After a rather long wait he was given another ship, an old one which he rebuilt and named the *Bon Homme Richard* to honor Benjamin Franklin. It was with the *Bon Homme Richard* that Jones fought the memorable battle against the British warship *Serapis*. He lashed his ship to the *Serapis,* and in the battle the *Bon Homme Richard* was on fire and filling with water, ripping apart, when the British captain asked if Jones was ready to surrender. His answer has rung through the centuries: "Sir, I have not yet begun to fight." Then he and his men boarded the *Serapis* and captured her while his own boat sank. In France he was given a hero's welcome for this victory, but somehow in the colonies it was ignored.

After the Revolution, Jones was sent to Europe to collect prize money owed to the United States. In 1788 he accepted Catherine the Great's invitation to become a Russian rear admiral. He was successful against the Turks, but political intrigue prevented him from getting the credit he was due. Jones was discharged from the Russian navy and returned to Paris. He died there in the middle of the French Revolution.

Although John Paul Jones is generally considered the founder of the American naval tradition, his grave was forgotten until 1905, when the American ambassador to France discovered it and had the remains brought to Annapolis, where they are enshrined in a crypt at the U.S. Naval Academy.

General Friedrich von Steuben

WARREN WHEELOCK

Bronze
Height: 9'6"
Base: granite (7'7")

Installed 1947

Baron von Steuben was an aide to Frederick the Great and a brilliant reformer and trainer in the Prussian army, but he lost the royal favor. In 1777, while in Paris, he was persuaded to take a position instructing the Continental Army in America. Here he was given the title of Inspector General by the Congress.

He spent the bitter winter of 1777–78 in Valley Forge, sharing the sufferings of the ill-fed and ill-tended men as he organized and disciplined them into a powerful striking force.

Friedrich von Steuben gave his fortune in the service of the young United States and was finally repaid by a pension voted by Congress and large tracts of land granted by various states.

Marquis de Lafayette

RAOUL JOSSET

Bronze
Height: 10'5"
Base: granite (7'6")

Installed 1947

A young French general and statesman, Lafayette had inherited a fortune from his family. When he heard about the American Declaration of Independence and the disasters suffered by the patriot army in New Jersey, he enthusiastically decided to help. Although he had been forbidden by the French Court, which wanted to appear neutral, he outfitted a ship and set sail for America. He took the chance of losing his title and property by being arrested or captured by the British. When his ship reached North Carolina, he recruited one hundred men, equipped them with clothing and guns and came to Philadelphia to offer his services to the colonies.

In 1777, at the age of 20, Lafayette was appointed a major general, was wounded at Brandywine, shared the hardships of Valley Forge and later distinguished himself at Yorktown. In the march to Virginia, he saved an entire corps from falling apart by borrowing $10,000 from the merchants of Baltimore, on his own credit, to buy food and equipment.

When the war was over, Lafayette traveled abroad. He bought a large plantation in French Guiana, where he provided instruction for freed slaves. It was shortly after this, in 1789, that Lafayette created the modern French flag. After a falling out with the Jacobins, however, he was declared a traitor. He escaped but was caught and jailed in Austria for four years.

Long after his liberation, Lafayette declined honors from Napoleon and refused President Jefferson's offer of the governorship of Louisiana, but he accepted an invitation from the American Congress to visit the United States. Everywhere he went there were incredible celebrations, and Congress voted him $200,000 and a large tract of land in gratitude for his services to this country.

General Nathaniel Greene

LEWIS ISELIN JR.

Bronze
Height: 9'3"
Base: granite (7'1")

Installed 1961

Nathaniel Greene was born in Rhode Island, a descendant of Dr. John Greene, who helped Roger Williams found the state. He and his seven brothers worked hard on his father's farm, but he was determined to get an education, and he collected books and read widely while continuing to work. He saw the trouble with England coming, so he studied the art of war and joined the Kentish Guards. For this he was thrown out of his Quaker meeting.

In 1775, Greene was appointed brigadier general of the Rhode Island contingent of the Continental Army at Boston, and he won George Washington's confidence by the perfect discipline of his brigade.

Greene's campaign in South Carolina and Georgia ended the British domination. For this he was later given a fortune in money and estates by grateful southerners whose territory he had defended.

General Richard Montgomery

J. WALLACE KELLY

Bronze
Height: 9'6"
Base: granite (8')

Installed 1947

While he was in the British army, Irish-born Richard Montgomery distinguished himself in battle and rose to the rank of captain. At the close of the war with France he moved to England, but after ten years without a promotion he became bitter and sold his commission in the army. He immigrated to America, married, became politically active and in 1775 was commissioned one of eight brigadier generals in the army. During the Revolutionary War, Montgomery took his forces to Canada, where they captured Montreal. For this victory he was made a major general. But he decided to attack Quebec, saying that "until Quebec is taken, Canada is unconquered." Sad to say, he was killed instantly by cannon shot, and the British troops defeated his demoralized army. The British commander had him buried with military honors, and his body lay in Quebec for 42 years until, at the request of the New York legislature, it was brought back and buried in a New York City churchyard.

35

Below the terrace is an unusual fountain that merits a closer look.

Travertine marble

Philadelphia Museum of Art, West Approach
Dedicated 1926

Fountain of
the Seahorses

For the dedication of the *Fountain of the Seahorses* in 1926, 3,000 people gathered at the west facade of the new Art Museum, and the Navy Yard band played martial music. The Italian ambassador explained that the original fountain in Rome had been a kind of sacred emblem throughout the history of Italy. The original *Fontana dei Cavalli Marini* was installed in the Borghese Gardens in 1740 by order of Pope Clement XII. This copy was brought here by steamship in 76 pieces. In honor of the event, the Italian government designed a medal showing on one side the *Santa Maria,* flagship of Columbus, and on the other a low relief of this fountain, a gift in commemoration of the 150th anniversary of American independence.

36

Proceeding around the fountain and back up the steps on the west side of the terrace, we again pass the statues of Lafayette, Greene and Montgomery before climbing the steps to the west entrance to the museum.

Greeting us with open hand is the seated figure of John Marshall. When the justice died in 1835, the Liberty Bell was rung in his honor, and it began to crack.

Bronze
Height: 6′8″
Base: granite (5′6″)

Philadelphia Museum of Art, West Entrance
Installed 1931

Chief Justice John Marshall

WILLIAM WETMORE STORY

The founder of judicial review and of the American system of constitutional law, John Marshall was born in a log cabin in the Virginia frontier. There, in a homespun environment with fourteen brothers and sisters, he learned to be thrifty, and throughout his life he dressed in a plain manner.

At Valley Forge, Marshall was an officer in the Continental Army under Washington and when the war was over, he became a lawyer and a political figure. Washington offered him the position of Attorney General, which he declined. When John Adams became president, however, he appointed Marshall Secretary of State and then Chief Justice of the Supreme Court of the United States. For a while he held both positions at the same time.

John Marshall's career was so illustrious that in 1901, on the 100th anniversary of the day he took his seat on the bench of the Supreme Court, judicial business stopped all over the country. The president, Congress and the Supreme Court, along with state, city and county bar associations, colleges, law schools and public schools, celebrated the day with appropriate exercises.

This sculpture is a copy of the one on the grounds of the Capitol building in Washington, D.C., which was done by the son of Joseph Story in 1884. Story was an associate justice on the Supreme Court and the author of *Commentaries on the Constitution of the United States*, which he dedicated to Marshall.

Story's son, William Wetmore Story, was a successful young lawyer, but he was talented as well in painting, sculpture, music and poetry. When Justice Story died, his son was asked to design a marble memorial for him. This changed his life. He gave up his legal career and went to Italy to learn to sculpt. After completing some works here in America, he settled in Italy for the rest of his life.

In the 1920s, as a gift of Congressman James Beck, a plaster replica was commissioned of the Washington, D.C., statue, and a Philadelphia sculptor, Louis Milione, was employed to oversee the casting in bronze. In 1931, it was placed on its granite base at the Art Museum's west entrance.

37

Looking to the left of the museum doors, we can see a group of large figures by Sir Jacob Epstein.

Bronze
Height: 12′2″
Weight: 13 tons
Base: granite (2′3½″)

Philadelphia Museum of Art, West Entrance
Unveiled 1955

Social Consciousness

SIR JACOB EPSTEIN

Jacob Epstein was no stranger to controversy. For fifty years his works were attacked by English art critics who sometimes called them "vile" and "obscene." His works were striking in effect and different from those that were in style at the time. Born in New York, Epstein lived in Europe most of his life, and this commission from the Fairmount Park Art Association meant a return to his native land.

When this piece arrived, it was set temporarily on the west terrace of the Art Museum while its permanent site was readied. When Epstein saw the proposed site on the east bank of the Schuylkill, he said it was ugly and would prefer to see his work remain where it was.

The three bronze statues in the group are entitled *Compassion, Mother Eternal* (seated) and *Succor*. "*Compassion*," Epstein wrote, "is a great consoler, a gentle and saving hand extended to help the afflicted and downhearted of the world." On the right, he explained, "is man-child returning to its eternal mother, which is Mother Earth. It encompasses life and death." Epstein added that he believes everyone will understand the symbolism of social consciousness in these figures.

In 1955, when this work was unveiled, there were outcries from a veterans' organization and snide comments from newspaper reporters and other observers. It would be interesting to see how these views have changed since that time.

38

Across the entrance on the east side of the museum doors is a work by Louise Nevelson, the best-known woman sculptor in this statuary tour. Nevelson was in her seventies when she created this large piece.

Corten steel
Height: 18'3"
Length: 10'
Width: 5'
Weight: 18,000 lbs.
Base: plywood

Philadelphia Museum of Art, West Entrance
Installed 1974

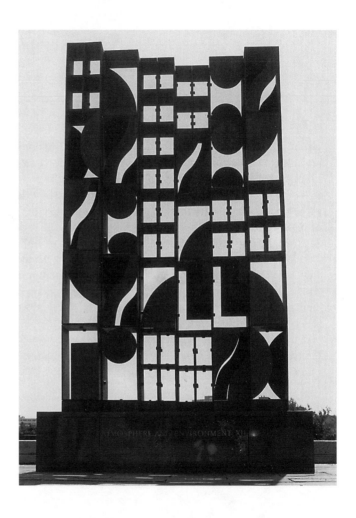

Atmosphere and Environment, XII

LOUISE NEVELSON

Corten steel is the metal used in making railroad freight cars. There is no paint or other finish on this work because it was designed to rust and form its own protective shield, much like the green patina formed by the oxidation of copper and bronze. *Atmosphere and Environment, XII* consists of six columns of five cubes, all bolted together.

Louise Nevelson grew up in Maine, where her father had a lumber business. Perhaps that childhood environment influenced her to use scraps of wood in her assemblages.

In 1971, this work was purchased by the Fairmount Park Art Association after it had been exhibited in France and in front of the Seagram Building in New York. Nevelson felt that it should be located among tall buildings. When it was installed here in 1974, a newspaper reporter wise-cracked, "That isn't a pile of orange crates stacked up on the plaza behind the Philadelphia Museum of Art." Another wrote, "Her sculpture is dominated by her eye for the placement of details: It's either instantaneously right or it's not."

39 *We now proceed around the museum and approaching the front, we encounter the statue of General Anthony Wayne, gleaming in the light. Louis Ewald, the artist who gilded this work, also gilded our Joan of Arc.*

Gilded bronze
Height: 12'
Base: granite (13½')

Philadelphia Museum of Art, East Terrace
Installed June 16, 1938

General Anthony Wayne

JOHN GREGORY

This statue, Philadelphia's first monument to "Mad Anthony Wayne," took thirty years to be erected. In 1905, some of the members of the Penn Club, an old and distinguished Philadelphia group, conceived the idea of a memorial to honor this much-admired Revolutionary War general. They raised funds and carefully secured them so that they could be used only for this purpose.

It so happened that one of the members of this memorial committee was then the governor of Pennsylvania. He argued that the statue should be placed in Valley Forge Park, but the other members wanted it to be in Philadelphia. So the money lay in the bank collecting interest while the governor, using state funds, had another statue made and placed in Valley Forge.

In 1930, the Pennsylvania chapter of the Sons of the American Revolution decided to raise $150,000 for a General Wayne statue, and the original funds were added to this sum. The new committee took great pains to use an expert on the Colonial period to ensure that the clothes on the figure were authentic, and they called a veterinarian to make certain that the horse used for the model was the special type of thoroughbred black stallion that the general always rode.

In the dedication ceremony, Wayne was described as one of the greatest maneuvering tacticians. Always in the heat of every action, he chose the post of greatest danger, exhibiting a boldness that gained him the universal affection of his troops. His reckless courage earned him the title "Mad Anthony."

John Gregory of New York, one of the country's best-known sculptors, was given the commission to do the models for the statue. It was reported that the work was a critical success, that it was "very characteristic" of Wayne as a young officer and that "the action of the horse is notable and beautiful from the fact that he seems to touch the ground so lightly."

The base was designed by the Philadelphia architect Paul P. Cret, who wanted its black granite to contrast with the gold finial on the roof of the museum.

In 1968, Louis Ewald, a 76-year-old Bryn Athyn artist, gilded the statue. It took six weeks to size in place more than 4,700 squares of gold leaf at a cost of $6,000.

Straight ahead, in the center of the East Court, is a circular fountain honoring Henry M. Phillips, one of the members appointed to the original board of the Fairmount Park Commission and one of its earliest presidents.

We now remember a statue that is no longer here.

Bronze
Height: 8'6"
Base: bronze

Sports Complex, South Philadelphia

Rocky

A. THOMAS SCHOMBERG

For a short time, *Rocky* was on the Parkway. The Philadelphia Art Commission rejected the sculptor's idea that the *Rocky* statue be placed permanently atop the steps of the Philadelphia Museum of Art. The Commission declared that the figure of the boxer from the movie *Rocky* was too commercial to remain, but that it could stay until the moviemakers finished shooting *Rocky III*. In the original movie, Sylvester Stallone, who plays the hero, runs up the steps of the museum as part of his homemade training plan. After seeing the movie, many people would also run up the steps and, at the top, raise their arms in victory like their hero. Stallone, who had offered the statue to the city as a gift, felt hurt by its rejection and said that he would ship it back to California. There was much discussion in the city, some people calling the statue a "movie prop" and some demanding that it be left on the steps of the Art Museum permanently.

Tom Schomberg, the sculptor, said of the controversy, "I am confident that the piece . . . holds as much power esthetically as any piece in that [museum] courtyard." Ruth Seltzer, the late newspaper society columnist, said that the statue expresses an "indomitable spirit of man."

Schomberg, a former basketball player turned sports sculptor, said that our preoccupation with sports makes us "in a way like reincarnated Romans. . . . Our athletes are modern-day gladiators." The A. Thomas Schomberg Foundry cast the "Rocky" figure. Other statues of athletes by Schomberg have been installed at the Astrodome, the Superdome and Yankee Stadium.

Rocky is now ensconced with other real and fictional sports heroes at the Spectrum in the Sports Complex in South Philadelphia.

40

Perched on the museum's front steps is the famous depiction of Prometheus by Jacques Lipchitz. According to Greek myth, Prometheus was a Titan who stole fire from heaven and gave it to man. For this he was punished by Zeus by being chained to a rock, where a vulture tore at his liver each day. Legend has it that Hercules saved Prometheus, but in the Lipchitz version, Prometheus strangles the tormenting bird himself.

Bronze
Height: 8'
Base: stone

Philadelphia Museum of Art, East Court Steps
Installed 1952

Prometheus Strangling the Vulture

JACQUES LIPCHITZ

In 1941, after living in constant fear for his life, Jacques Lipchitz escaped to America from war-ravaged Europe. He had been part of the Paris art scene for thirty years, and his unusual concept of Prometheus dates back to 1933. He was quoted as saying, "The idea of a struggle between light and darkness, between good and evil, is an idea always present in my work." Through the years Lipchitz made several sketches of his Prometheus and eventually produced a plaster cast which in 1952 won a medal in a show at the Pennsylvania Academy of the Fine Arts in Philadelphia. The day after that exhibition, his studio in New York, containing a great part of his life's work, was destroyed by fire (the very element that the mythical Prometheus had given to mankind).

Luck did not totally desert Lipchitz, however, because the Philadelphia Museum of Art bought the piece that was here in the art show, paying the largest sum for it that they had ever given a living sculptor for a single work of art. His comment, quoted after the fire and the purchase, was, "to rise like a Phoenix from one's own ashes is a painfully joyous experience."

41

Now look up to the museum's north pediment, the only one to be completed with sculpture. From the ground it is difficult to believe that these figures are life-size.

Polychrome and gold glazes on terra cotta
Height: 12′ at center
Width: 70′ at base

Philadelphia Museum of Art, East Plaza
Installed 1932

The North Pediment

PAUL JENNEWEIN

There may be nothing else quite like the great North Pediment anywhere in the world. Paul Jennewein, the sculptor, created the life-size gods for the tympanum in 1932. The Philadelphia Museum of Art was the first contemporary building of classical design to display in exterior decoration the rediscovered polychrome of the Greeks. John Gregory, who was the creator of the famous panels for the Folger Shakespeare Library in Washington, D.C., made models for the figures that were to go into the south and center pediments. However, the only company that could produce these figures went out of business, so the models are still in storage.

The thirteen mythological figures, according to the sculptor, are a representation of sacred and profane love, the two underlying forces that are basic to the development of art and civilization in every age. They symbolize the influences that produced Western culture.

The central figure, the creative force of man, is Zeus or Jupiter. To the right of Zeus is Demeter or Ceres, the goddess of law and order and of marriage and peaceful life. Next is the child Triptolemus, representing the returning life cycle, then Ariadne, sitting at the foot of the laurel, followed by a kneeling Theseus slaying the Minotaur.

On the left of Zeus is Venus, the goddess of love and beauty, and Cupid, the god of love, showing the lion to the kneeling Adonis. Aurora, the goddess of dawn, turns from the owl, the bird of night.

42

Coming down the museum's front steps, we see a plinth on our left supporting The Amazon *by August Kiss. Kiss became famous in Europe for creating the original of this work. A copy of it was carved in marble for King Ludwig I of Bavaria. On the right is* The Lion Fighter *by Albert Wolff. Wolff was among the leading German sculptors of his time.*

Philadelphia Museum of Art
East Entrance
Installed 1929

The Amazon

AUGUST KISS

The Lion Fighter

ALBERT WOLFF

Bronze
Height: 11′3″
Base: limestone (17′)

August Kiss completed work on *The Amazon* in 1837. It was cast in bronze and installed in front of the National Museum in Berlin. Eighteen years later, Albert Wolff, another Berlin artist who had studied with Kiss under the same teacher, produced *The Lion Fighter,* and it was placed near *The Amazon* as a companion piece.

Bronze
Height: 14′
Base: limestone (17′)

In 1889 the Fairmount Park Art Association acquired the original plaster casts of both works. *The Lion Fighter* was cast in bronze in 1892 and exhibited at the 1893 Columbian Exposition. Later it was placed in front of the Post Office at Ninth and Chestnut Streets. Although the plaster *Amazon* was exhibited for a while, the Art Association decided in 1909 that it would commission only American art and sent the piece to Harvard's Germanic Museum. In 1928, however, with the Benjamin Franklin Parkway nearing completion and the Museum of Art being built, the Association arranged to have *The Amazon* cast in bronze. Then both sculptures were installed, as they are in Berlin, in front of a splendid museum.

43 *We have a long walk now across the street, around the fountains and back down to the Eakins Oval. We cross to the south side of the Parkway and continue until we approach the statue of General Francisco de Miranda.*

Bronze
Height: 15'
Base: granite

Benjamin Franklin Parkway at 20th Street
Unveiled July 1977

General Francisco de Miranda

CARMELO TOBACCO

One art critic was rather bitter when he reported that with the installation of this figure yet another replica sculpture had been added to the public works on the Parkway. He felt that modern artists should be allowed to express original ideas instead of copying existing statuary.

This statue of Francisco de Miranda, a Venezuelan patriot who fought with the American army in the Revolutionary War, is a copy of the one given to France by Venezuela in the 1920s. The original stands in Valmy battlefield near Paris and was sculpted by Lorenzo Gonzalez. Our figure was done by Carmelo Tobacco, who was born in Italy but lived in Caracas, Venezuela. It is said that another cast will be made for Caracas.

44

Continuing along the Parkway and around Logan Circle, we come on the right to a large bronze globe directly opposite the entrance to the Franklin Institute. This is Paul Manship's Aero Memorial. *Another Manship sculpture can be found in Rittenhouse Square. It is a graceful bronze entitled* Duck Girl. *When Manship was 24 he won the Prix de Rome, which included three years of study at the American Academy in Rome. This experience had a great influence on his style. The Minnesota Museum of Art in St. Paul has more than 300 Manship works.*

Bronze
Height: 8′
Base: granite (9′8″)

Logan Circle at 20th Street
Dedicated June 1, 1950

Aero Memorial

PAUL MANSHIP

After World War I the Aero Club of Pennsylvania conceived the plan to build a monument as a memorial to Pennsylvania aviators who had lost their lives in the war. It wasn't accomplished until after World War II, so they dedicated it to the fliers lost in both wars.

The sphere depicts the constellations in their relative positions. The signs of the zodiac and the mythological figures symbolize the men who have been carried across the heavens on wings. The access is set at an angle aimed at the North Star and the globe is mounted on ball bearings that allow it to be rotated.

The *Aero Memorial* was funded by donations that were matched by the Fairmount Park Art Association. The total cost came to about $35,000.

In the 1920s and 1930s, Paul Manship, the sculptor, enjoyed fame and fortune. He became one of the world's most successful artists. He was earning $75,000 for a piece of sculpture when artists working for the government's WPA program were being paid $35 a week.

Manship had requests to design medallions and garden sculptures and to do portraits of celebrities like John Barrymore. He received honors and awards and enough wealth to buy five townhouses in Manhattan, although he lived primarily in Europe. In Rockefeller Plaza in New York is Manship's gilded *Prometheus Fountain,* and at Radio City is his flying *Prometheus*. He also did the gates for the New York Zoo, the Woodrow Wilson Memorial for the League of Nations in Geneva and sculptures for the 1939 New York World's Fair.

45

Near the Aero Memorial *is the new site of this memorial.*

Bronze and granite
Height: 21′6″
Width: 17′
Depth: 13′

Benjamin Franklin Parkway at 20th
Street
Dedicated 1934
Rededicated November 11, 1994
(Veterans Day)

All Wars Memorial to Colored Soldiers and Sailors

J. OTTO SCHWEIZER

After 60 years of semi-obscurity in Fairmount Park, this statue was moved to a prominent position on the Benjamin Franklin Parkway.

With an elaborate parade of marchers, including war veterans, members of Masonic orders and children in drill teams, this heroic monument was rededicated on November 11, 1994. The gray-haired woman who unveiled it on that day had unveiled it the first time when she was a little girl. At that time she was given the honor because she was the granddaughter of Samuel Beecher Hart, the state legislator who fought to have this memorial built.

In 1927 the Swiss-born sculptor J. Otto Schweizer was commissioned by the Pennsylvania legislature to create a monument to honor the men who fought and died for our country. The figures he designed were of actual persons he knew. The edifice portrays six soldiers and sailors grouped around a figure of Justice beneath a symbolic Torch of Life that is guarded by four American eagles.

46 *We now proceed around Logan Circle, past the Moore College of Art, to the statue of Dr. Joseph Leidy in front of the Academy of Natural Sciences. The sculptor, Samuel Murray, was a Philadelphian who studied with Thomas Eakins at the Art Students League. Another of his works in Philadelphia is the statue of Commodore Barry in Independence Square. Murray also completed ten colossal figures of biblical prophets for the Witherspoon Building.*

Bronze
Height: 8'6"
Base: granite (10')

Benjamin Franklin Parkway at 19th and Race Streets
Originally unveiled 1907
Installed 1930

Joseph Leidy

SAMUEL MURRAY

As often happens with public works of art, there was controversy as to where this statue should be placed. The Leidy Memorial Committee of Representative Citizens, who had raised $10,000 for the project, favored City Hall Plaza, but many of Leidy's friends and admirers preferred the Academy site. The committee won and in 1907, Samuel Murray's figure of Joseph Leidy was installed in City Hall Plaza. In 1930, however, the other side had its day when work was begun on realigning the Market Street subway tracks under City Hall. Leidy's statue was removed to its present location and placed on a new granite base.

When Joseph Leidy was a boy, he liked to wander along the rivers in Philadelphia to collect plants and minerals and make drawings of them. When he grew up, he became a physician, but after practicing for two years he turned to research and teaching, becoming known as the foremost American anatomist of his time. His insatiable interest in science included research in zoology, geology, botany, mineralogy and parasitology, in the study of which he discovered the identity of the worm that causes trichinosis in man.

Leidy became a pioneer in the study of paleontology, showing through fossil remains the one-time presence on this continent of the lion, tiger, camel, horse and rhinoceros. In 1858, he identified North America's first known dinosaur from bones discovered in Haddonfield, New Jersey. They can be seen today in the Academy of Natural Sciences.

For almost forty years, until his death in 1891, Leidy was a professor of anatomy at the University of Pennsylvania. For the last fifteen years of his life he taught natural history at Swarthmore College, and for ten years he served as president of the Academy of Natural Sciences and the Wagner Free Institute of Science.

47

A short distance away, near the entrance to the Academy of Natural Sciences, is the Academy's signature statue.

Bronze
Height: 14′
Base: granite (11′)

Benjamin Franklin Parkway at
19th Street
Installed April 1987

Deinonychus

KENT ULLBERG

Deinonychus antirrhopus was a dinosaur that lived 100 million years ago in the early Cretaceous Period. A skeleton of this species was discovered in Montana in 1964 by John Ostrom of Yale University. In 1969, Professor Ostrom published his theory that *Deinonychus* may have been warm-blooded, challenging the commonly held belief that dinosaurs, like reptiles, were cold-blooded. These fierce meat-eaters were nine feet long and four feet tall, and probably hunted in packs like wolves.

Kent Ullberg, an internationally honored sculptor, chose to represent *Deinonychus* because it reflected new scientific knowledge and it was found in America. The Academy of Natural Sciences, long known for its dinosaur research, now has its signature statue.

48

Now we are ready to give full attention to the wonderful fountain in Logan Circle.

Bronze
Height: 11'
Base: granite (5'2")
Basin circumference: 142'

Logan Circle
Opened to the public 1924

Swann Memorial Fountain

ALEXANDER STIRLING CALDER

Swann Memorial Fountain is in Logan Circle. Logan Circle is in the center of Logan Square. It is not so surprising, then, to hear it referred to as "Logan Circle Fountain." It is also known as "Fountain of the Three Rivers," and it was built in 1920 with funds left by the widow of Dr. Wilson Cary Swann, former head of the Philadelphia Fountain Society.

Around the basin of the fountain are large sculptures of frogs and turtles with open mouths spouting sprays that arch over the central figures. Philadelphia's three rivers are represented. The Delaware River, being the largest of the three, is shown as a man's figure. A woman holding the neck of a swan represents the next-largest river, the Schuylkill, and a young woman leaning against a swan symbolizes the Wissahickon Creek. The sculptor's daughter wrote that her father had placed the swans in the fountain as a visual pun on the name of the donor.

Sculptor Alexander Stirling Calder was the only one of the six sons of Alexander Milne Calder to choose a career in art. As a youngster he helped out as his father and a large staff worked on the hundreds of sculptures for City Hall. As a young man he was awarded commissions for colossal sculptures in buildings, parks and gardens all over the United States. We in Philadelphia are fortunate to have so many of his masterpieces. His son, Alexander Calder, was the famous designer of mobiles, stabiles and wire art.

Since this fountain is so involved with the name "Logan," it seems appropriate to include a description of the man behind the name. James Logan came to Philadelphia with William Penn in 1699. He made a fortune in the Susquehanna fur trade and in land speculation. He also spent years in public service as a member of the provincial council, mayor of Philadelphia, Chief Justice of the Pennsylvania Supreme Court and, in 1736, acting governor of the province. In addition, he was the inventor of the Conestoga (covered) wagon and, of all things, storm windows. Logan, a self-taught scholar, had the finest collection of books in the colonies. When he died he left them to the city.

49

Crossing the street, we now walk along past the Four Seasons Hotel to the commanding figure of General Kosciuszko. When the general died in 1817, a few Polish peasants came to the field near Krakow where his little army had bravely battled Russian artillery. Lacking the means to build him a monument, they simply brought some earth from their own village. Word of this act spread through Poland and streams of people brought soil from their villages to deposit in the field. The result was a mountain over 200 feet high composed of the Polish soil for which Kosciuszko fought and died.

Bronze
Height: 12'
Base: white marble and red granite (8')

Benjamin Franklin Parkway at 18th Street
Installed July 3, 1979

General Tadeusz Kosciuszko

MARIAN KONIECZNY

The amazing story of Tadeusz Kosciuszko deserves a lot more space than is possible here. He came to Philadelphia from Poland at the age of 30 to volunteer in the Continental Army. Because he had studied military engineering in Europe, he was given the rank of Colonel of Engineers.

During the Revolutionary War, Kosciuszko's special talent—the brilliant use of natural sites for fortifications and defense—produced successful strategies. His forts on the Delaware saved Philadelphia. Then he made a trap for the British in the Hudson Valley, forcing them to retreat to Saratoga, where General Burgoyne surrendered 6,000 soldiers. This first major victory of the war convinced Spain and France that the Continental Army could win, and they came to the aid of the colonies. Kosciuszko's most famous feat was the creation of West Point. By picking the one place where the Hudson River bends around a hill, he was able to build an impenetrable fortress, and the British never dared to attack it. They had to change their entire plan of warfare. When the United States Military Academy was established at West Point in 1802, the first monument built was a tribute to Kosciuszko.

Stories told about the Polish hero show him to have had an almost saintly character. He gave his own food ration to hungry British prisoners of war and to sick men in the army hospital. Once, when his fellow officers gave him a slave as a gift, he said he had no idea of what to do with a slave. He was told that he could do whatever he wished, so he turned to the slave and told him he was a free man.

Kosciuszko was so modest that he never asked for honors and actually declined promotions in the army, but when the war was over, a grateful Congress made him a brigadier general. He then went back to Poland, which soon after was under attack by Russia, Prussia and Austria. He trained a militia and fought gallantly as its commander, but was severely injured and imprisoned in Russia for two years. The czar then offered to release him, but he refused to go free unless 12,000 captive Poles were also freed. The czar agreed on the condition that he never return to Poland.

Kosciuszko had become a worldwide hero, but he was sad at heart and paralyzed from his wounds when he sailed to Philadelphia in 1797. Here he received a resounding welcome. His admirers unhitched the horses from his carriage and pulled it themselves through the cheering crowds. Many distinguished statesmen paid visits to his house at Third and Pine Streets. George Washington gave him the highest accolades. He presented General Kosciuszko with his sword and another prized possession, the ring of the Society of the Cincinnati. His close friend Thomas Jefferson became executor of his will, which left his American assets to be used to purchase the freedom of slaves and to furnish them with land and education.

The Kosciuszko statue was a Bicentennial gift from the people of Poland. The red and white base symbolizes the colors of the Polish flag. It was placed diagonally across from the monument to the Polish astronomer Copernicus. Marian Konieczny, the statue's sculptor, was the president of the Academy of Fine Arts in Krakow, Poland.

50

Continue following the Parkway to Cherry Street. Here is another of the many fountains that are so refreshing to see in the city.

Bronze
Height: 26′
Base: stone

Cherry Street and Benjamin Franklin Parkway
Installed 1965

The Tuscan Girl Fountain

OSCAR STONOROV AND JORIS VIVARELLI

Oscar Stonorov was quoted as saying that the *Tuscan Girl Fountain* "shows the exuberance of adolescents frolicking under a waterfall." John Canaday, a *New York Times* art critic, wrote that "it is the worst single sculpture of the 20th century."

Stonorov, in collaboration with Joris Vivarelli of Florence, Italy, designed the fountain, which is one of five fountain sculptures in less than a mile on the Parkway.

The fountain was executed in Italy and shipped to the United States in three sections. It was welded together on the site. Water falls onto its figures from a reflecting pool and is continuously recirculated. The Philadelphia *Bulletin* wrote that there was a swimming pool on the roof of the hotel adjoining the fountain and the tanned face of a bather would occasionally appear over the wall, adding a real-life quality to the bronze juveniles below.

Oscar Stonorov was an architect who had a passion for revitalizing cities, and he took great interest in the social and political events in Philadelphia.

51

Proceeding one more block to 16th Street, we come to Nathan Rapoport's memorial to the victims of the Holocaust. "Never forget" is the motto of those who survived. Every year services of remembrance are held here.

Bronze
Height: 18′
Base: black granite

Benjamin Franklin Parkway at 16th Street
Presented April 26, 1964

The Holocaust Memorial:
Monument to the Six Million Jewish Martyrs

NATHAN RAPOPORT

The Association of Jewish New Americans is a group that began with 400 families, many of whom fled Poland after World War II. The Association, together with the Federation of Jewish Agencies of Greater Philadelphia, presented this sculpture to the city as a tribute to those who perished in the Holocaust and as a reminder of this tragedy in the struggle for the freedom and dignity of mankind. The memorial portrays a dying mother lying amid flames, a child holding up the Torah scroll containing the five books of Moses, a patriarchal figure with his arms raised in benediction and other arms holding daggers, representing Jewish resistance. All of these are enveloped in flames from a burning bush, and at the top is a branched candelabrum, or menorah.

Sculptor Nathan Rapoport, a native of Warsaw, also designed the world-famous monument that stands on the site of the Warsaw Ghetto, where 350,000 Jews were slaughtered by the Nazis. Philadelphia, with its history as the birthplace of American freedom, was chosen as an appropriate location for this monument symbolizing triumph over suffering and bondage.

52

We come now to City Hall, certainly the largest and most amazing mass of sculpture in the city. Of all its features, the great surmounting figure of William Penn is easily the grandest. It is the one Philadelphia statue that cannot be missed and will never be forgotten.

Bronze
Height: 37′
Weight: 26½ tons

City Hall Tower
Installed November 25, 1894

William Penn

ALEXANDER MILNE CALDER

The famous statue of William Penn was cast by a crew of skilled metal workers brought here from Europe in 1892. It was cast in 47 pieces, and as each piece was finished it was placed in a nearby field. There, neighborhood children delighted in walking on the brim of Penn's hat, which is 23 feet around. His nose is 13 inches long and his coat cuffs three feet long. Over a period of six months all the pieces were hauled by horse teams to the City Hall courtyard, where they were assembled and remained on display for a year. Then they were separated into fourteen sections and hoisted up the tower for slow assembly.

Some people thought the statue a monstrosity, and sculptor Alexander Milne Calder was quoted as complaining that the architect in charge of installation disliked it and placed it facing northeast rather than south so that Penn's face would be hidden by shadows most of the day. Others say that the statue was set to look toward the site where Penn signed his famous treaty with the Indians in 1682. Liked or not, Penn's statue has become a symbol of Philadelphia and a member of its family.

In every nook and corner of City Hall there are interesting and often curious sculptures designed by Calder and his staff, and although some are of an enormous size, they are hard to see without binoculars because City Hall is 548 feet high. Calder left other contributions to Philadelphia and the world, most notably his son, Alexander Stirling Calder, and his grandson, Alexander Calder, both great artists in their own right.

The
Kelly Drive
Sculptures

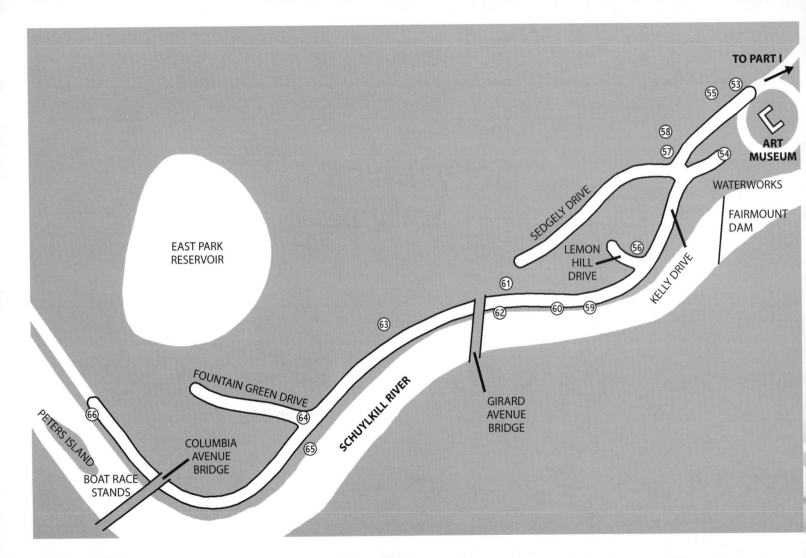

PART II   THE KELLY DRIVE SCULPTURES

On this tour it is safer to stay on the sidewalk on the south side of Kelly Drive because of the car traffic. Crossing the highway requires extreme caution. Or, if traveling by car, there are some parking areas along the way.

53

This first sculpture on the north side of Kelly Drive, between the Philadelphia Museum of Art and Sedgeley Drive, is sometimes hidden by shrubbery.

Bronze
Height: 2′5″
Base: stone

Across from Azalea Garden
Installed 1965

Tiger at Bay

ALBINO MANCA

On a list of top things to see in New York City is Albino Manca's World War II monument, the *East Coast Memorial* in Battery Park. It is a giant bronze diving eagle 18 feet high.

Manca was born in Sardinia, Italy. He studied and then taught at the Royal Academy of Fine Arts in Rome and came to the United States in 1938. He cast bronze portrait busts of Metropolitan Opera stars and also became recognized for animal bronzes. He produced the Pietà medal sold at the Vatican pavilion of the New York World's Fair in 1964 and Robert Moses' low relief in marble at Fordham University's Lincoln Center campus.

Manca's *Tiger at Bay* was exhibited at the Pennsylvania Academy of the Fine Arts before the Fairmount Park Art Association had it installed in this park.

54

We walk to our left into the Azalea Garden, where the figure of a powerful cat seems to be patiently waiting.

Marble
Height: 5′1″
Base: granite

Azalea Garden, off Kelly Drive
Installed 1954

Puma

WILLIAM ZORACH

Whether or not the flowers are blooming, it is worth walking into the Azalea Garden to see *Puma*. It is carved in smooth black marble and sits on a granite base looking mysterious.

The sculptor of this beautiful cat, William Zorach, abandoned a promising career as a painter in oils in order to devote most of his time to sculpture. He brought to his work the best that Europe of the early 20th century and the ancients had to offer, and he expressed American conceptions of profound feelings for nature and life. He was the sculptor for the Post Office and the Department of Justice buildings in Washington, D.C. In New York he made an aluminum work called *Spirit of the Dance,* which was hung in Radio City Music Hall.

Zorach reintroduced the practice of direct carving on large blocks of stone and wood and had an enormous influence on his contemporaries and on younger sculptors. He believed in the values of the Art Students League of New York, and he was an outstanding teacher there from 1929 until his death in 1966.

55

Look across Kelly Drive on the north side to see a bronze representation of mythical figures.

Bronze
Height: 6′1″
Base: granite (4′3″)

Kelly Drive, north of Fairmount Avenue
Cast in France, 1885
Installed 1885

Silenus and the Infant Bacchus

ATTRIBUTED TO PRAXITELES

The fourth century B.C. is the only epoch in history referred to by the name of a sculptor. It is called the "Age of Praxiteles." Praxiteles was one of the most famous sculptors in ancient Greece, and his works are lost or known only by description or Roman copies. He liked to present youthful gods or beings with a joy of life. His *Silenus and the Infant Bacchus* depicts a handsome satyr gently holding the baby Bacchus. In Greek mythology, Bacchus grew up to become the god of wine. This statue was admired for its grace and the sculptor's skillful use of the tree trunk on which Silenus is leaning. Many copies were made of the original, and it is said that the best Roman copy was taken from Greece by the French and placed in the Louvre. It was from this replica that Philadelphia's bronze version was cast and bought by the Fairmount Park Art Association.

This statue thematically resembles one which is an undisputed original found in Olympia in 1877. It is a figure of Hermes with the infant Dionysus and is said to exhibit Praxiteles' supreme artistic skill and his unsurpassed handling of marble.

56

Continuing our sidewalk stroll, we pass a street called Waterworks Drive. It leads to the recently reconstructed Fairmount Waterworks, which is worth a tour of its own. This pumping system for Philadelphia's water supply was a famous engineering marvel when it opened in 1815 and operated for close to 100 years. It now will house a museum, a restaurant and farmers' markets.

Continuing on the path, we see across the road The Pilgrim.

Bronze
Height: 9'1"
Base: fieldstone (1'7")

Kelly Drive at Lemon Hill Drive
Installed 1904
Moved to present location 1920

The Pilgrim

AUGUSTUS SAINT-GAUDENS

Wearing a buckled hat, holding a Holy Bible in one hand and a cane in the other and with his cape surrounding him, *The Pilgrim* is a formidable figure.

The first version of this sculpture is called *The Puritan,* and it was installed in 1887 in Springfield, Massachusetts. Later the New England Society of Pennsylvania asked Saint-Gaudens to make a replica for Philadelphia. In the newer version, executed in 1904, the sculptor changed the facial features, the cloak, the legs, the left hand and the Bible. The figure stands in a confident manner on a rough-hewn stone pedestal with a concrete foundation. It is an example of the art of Saint-Gaudens near the end of a prolific and honored career. Shortly after the dedication of this sculpture, President Theodore Roosevelt, who admired ancient Greek coins, asked the sculptor to redesign the ten- and the twenty-dollar gold coins. For the twenty-dollar coin Saint-Gaudens created a figure of Liberty on the obverse and a flying eagle on the reverse side. This is known as the "Saint-Gaudens Gold Double Eagle" and is considered to be one of the most beautiful coins ever minted. It was issued for circulation from 1907 (a few months after the sculptor died) to 1933. In 1934, all but two of 455,500 double eagles that had been struck in 1933 but never circulated were melted down by order of president Franklin D. Roosevelt, a cousin of former president Teddy Roosevelt, their originator. This was the end of the creation of gold coins for circulation in the U.S. The two coins saved from being melted are now in the old Mint Collection of the Smithsonian Institution.

57

It is best to view the statue of Lincoln from a distance since the head is about 32 feet from the ground. Originally this monument was situated in the center of heavily traveled Kelly Drive. It was moved to this site for the safety of both the sculpture and the motorist.

Bronze
Height: 9′6″
Base: granite (22′6″)

Kelly Drive at Sedgely Drive
Installed 1871
Moved to present location 2002

Abraham Lincoln

RANDOLPH ROGERS

The sculptor, Randolph Rogers, convinced the committee members of Philadelphia's Lincoln Monument Association to accept a seated figure rather than the standing figure they had requested. In the sculptor's own words, "Mr. Lincoln in a sitting posture holding in one hand the Emancipation Proclamation, and a pen in the other, his eyes turned toward heaven, asking the Almighty his approval for the act. It was the great event of his life."

Rogers worked to achieve realism in the design of the president's clothes and the carvings on his chair. The pedestal has an eagle in each corner, a plaque of the coat of arms of Philadelphia on one side and garlands over crossed swords on the front. The inscription reads: "To Abraham Lincoln from a grateful people." An enthusiastic crowd of 50,000 attended the sculpture's dedication.

When Rogers was about 23 years old, he was enabled to study art in Italy, first in Florence and then in Rome. Five years later he returned to New York City and opened a studio. He received many commissions for portrait statues; he did one of William H. Seward. In 1858, he designed bronze doors for the U.S. Capitol in Washington, D.C. From 1860 on he lived in Italy and was an important figure in the American colony in Rome. He died there at the age of 67.

58

About 75 feet north of the Lincoln sculpture on the same grassy plot there is an unusual design.

Painted weathering steel
Height: 4'6"
Width: 20'
Depth: 20'

Kelly Drive at Sedgely Drive
Installed 1985

The Wedges

ROBERT MORRIS

Robert Morris has exhibited works of art in all parts of the world, from Argentina to Scandinavia. Some in permanent collections are in Melbourne, Australia; Stockholm, Sweden and a huge outdoor design called *Observatory* in Holland. In 1974 a large-scale maze was built, according to his plans, on the site of his show at the Institute of Contemporary Art (ICA) in Philadelphia.

Morris has taken part in many forms of art, from painting and writing to dance choreography and theater. In modern sculptural styles, he experimented with minimalism, conceptual art, action art and idea art. His work has been referred to as "ingenious."

The Wedges was donated to the Fairmount Park Art Association by Mr. and Mrs. H. Gates Lloyd in 1972.

Situated as it is back from the highway, the sculpture is easy to miss, but a 50-foot walk to its center brings a strange, isolated-from-the-world feeling. Its eight metal pieces enclose a space that seems to vibrate.

59

We walk on Boathouse Row to the statue of a hero of the Norsemen.

Bronze
Height: 7'4"
Base: granite (5'7")

Kelly Drive, north of Boathouse Row, near
Samuel Memorial
Installed c. 1918

Thorfinn Karlsefni

EINAR JONSSON

Einar Jonsson, the son of a farmer in Iceland, gained the chance to study art by attracting attention to his skill in woodcarving. A Reykjavik banker arranged for the 18-year-old Jonsson to go to Denmark and attend the Royal Academy of Fine Arts. Then he toured in European countries and stayed in Italy for two years. He made use of the legends of his country, aiming to reveal spiritual truths. In his own words, Jonsson said that his work is "built upon a personal philosophy of life. . . ."

When J. Bunford Samuel decided to commission the first of the sculptures his wife (Ellen Phillips Samuel) had provided for in her will, he asked the Scandinavian Foundation of New York for a suitable artist. They answered, "Jonsson."

So it was that Einar Jonsson got married in Iceland at the dock of the ship that brought him to the United States. He and his bride arrived in Philadelphia on a July day when the temperature was 87 degrees.

It was difficult at first, but they lived here two years while the statue was created. Jonsson chose the Icelandic hero Thorfinn Karlsefni because runic stones found and deciphered in Nova Scotia tell of Vikings landing there in 1007. Karlsefni was a Viking adventurer, supposedly the first to discover land in the Western Hemisphere.

Perhaps as a result of his being away from Iceland for two years in Philadelphia, Jonsson became even more valued in his home country. A beautiful museum was built in Reykjavik on a hill overlooking the port. It became his home and studio.

60

A little further along we come to the work of a sculptor who was famous for his portrayals of American Indians.

Bronze
Height: 7′6″
Base: granite (4′2″)

North of Boathouse Row, near Samuel Memorial
Installed 1887
Moved to present location 1985

Stone Age in America

JOHN J. BOYLE

In 1880, John J. Boyle spent two years in North Dakota among the Sioux Indians to prepare for a commission to sculpt *An Indian Family,* which went to Lincoln Park in Chicago.

The excellence of that work led to a commission to execute a similar group for the Fairmount Park Art Association. This time he modeled *The Stone Age in America,* and it has been called Boyle's masterpiece. It expresses the courage of an Indian mother, stone hatchet in hand, protecting her children from perhaps the mother of the dead bear cub at her feet. Boyle captures with marvelous modeling the animal skins the woman wore and the universal fight of human beings against their natural enemies. These figures bring ancient American history to life.

Boyle became a sculptor with a "full sense of the years of sacrifice and devotion necessary to succeed." As a boy he wanted to be a machinist but he became, first, an iron molder and then a stonecutter like several generations of his Irish father's family. It was a great discipline for a sculptor. In Philadelphia, he went evenings to Central High School and to the Franklin Institute drawing school and then he studied at the Pennsylvania Academy of the Fine Arts. When he was 26 years old, he went to Paris for three years and studied at the École des Beaux Arts.

There are other striking examples of Boyle's work in and around Philadelphia. A remarkable statue of Benjamin Franklin, which was a gift to the city from J. C. Strawbridge in 1898, was originally placed on the Post Office plaza. In 1938 the city gave it to the University of Pennsylvania, which Franklin had helped to found. The statue of John Christian Bullitt, which stands near City Hall, was executed by Boyle in 1902. He is represented as well in Washington, Chicago and New York City, but Philadelphia claims him as its own.

61

Walking on we come to a series of three terraces. Across from the terraces is the memorial to President Garfield.

Bronze
Height: 19′6″
Base: pink granite

Kelly Drive, south of Girard Avenue Bridge
Installed 1895

James A. Garfield Monument

AUGUSTUS SAINT-GAUDENS

In 1881, President James A. Garfield died from a shot fired by an irate job seeker. In 1889 the Fairmount Park Art Association chose Augustus Saint-Gaudens to create a memorial. The sculptor and his colleague Stanford White, an outstanding architect, came to Philadelphia and picked a site for the monument facing the Schuylkill River and opposite the Rond Point fountains.

When the statue was unveiled on the evening of Memorial Day, 1896, a sensational show of thousands of electric lights, boats lit with lanterns and fires along the river banks greeted the crowds who came to the ceremonies.

Saint-Gaudens and his family immigrated to New York City from Europe when he was six months old. When he completed grade school, he became an apprentice to a stone cameo cutter and he gained mastery over sculpture in low relief. At night he went to art classes. Then at the age of 19 he went to Paris, studied at the École des Beaux Arts and traveled to Italy, where he carved several marble figures. Then Saint-Gaudens returned to New York and opened a studio, completed many commissions and returned to Europe for two years, where he also had a studio. In 1881, he produced the Admiral Farragut memorial for New York and it brought him recognition and critical acclaim. He became an influential American talent, moving from stone carving to bronze casting. His work made him America's most important sculptor from the 1880s to his death in 1907.

In 1965, Cornish, New Hampshire, where Saint-Gaudens had a house and studio, was turned into a national historic site. In the Philadelphia Museum of Art we have his version of Diana, the goddess of the hunt, which originally was placed at Madison Square Garden in New York and was there for 34 years before a fire caused it to be moved to Philadelphia.

Ellen Phillips Samuel Memorial

KELLY DRIVE

62

Perhaps it was Ellen Phillips Samuel's uncle who inspired her to establish a fund that would develop this memorial. Her uncle, Henry W. Phillips, was a member of the Fairmount Park Commission when it was created in 1867 and was its president from 1881 to his death in 1884. He left a fund for a fountain, which was built at the entrance to the Philadelphia Museum of Art. Although Mrs. Samuel and her husband, J. Bunford Samuel, were charitable during their lifetimes, when she died she left an extraordinary will putting her residual estate in trust to the Fairmount Park Art Association with the funds to become available after the death of her husband. Her intention was for the money to be used for sculptures symbolizing the history of the settlement of America from earliest times. When she chose the site of the East River Drive (now Kelly Drive) it was mainly a walking path, not a highway, but the sculpture gardens that were later designed are an oasis of tranquility despite the modern traffic.

It was decided to create three terraces, each with its own theme, and to have international sculpture exhibitions to select the artists. The first competition was held in 1933, and 364 statues by 105 sculptors were shown. The Central Terrace was constructed first, and its themes were America's westward expansion and emigration from the rest of the world.

The second competition, in 1940, was affected by the war in Europe, so the international entries were limited to those already in the United States. Then, when America entered the war, construction on the memorial slowed. The South Terrace's themes were the development of the United States as a democracy and the growth of the eastern states.

In 1949 the third international sculpture competition was held and more than 250,000 people came to see the 252 works exhibited. This time some statues were bought for other sites. The North Terrace was the final construction of the memorial, and the selected art was to express the spiritual strengths of the nation. After 28 years, Mrs. Samuel's great gift came to fruition.

CENTRAL TERRACE

The Spirit of Enterprise (installed 1960 in North Terrace, relocated 1986 to Central Terrace)
Jacques Lipchitz
Bronze on granite base

Spanning the Continent (1937, installed 1938)
Robert Laurent
Bronze on granite base

The Ploughman (1938)
J. Wallace Kelly
Limestone on limestone base

The Miner (1938)
John B. Flannagan
Limestone on limestone base

The Slave (1940)
Helene Sardeau
Limestone on limestone base

Immigrant (1940)
Heinz Warneke
Limestone on limestone base

Welcoming to Freedom (1939)
Maurice Sterne
Bronze on granite

The theme is the spanning of the continent, the freeing of the slaves and the welcoming of immigrants.

SOUTH TERRACE

Settling of the Seaboard (1942)
Wheeler Williams
Limestone on granite base

The Puritan and the Quaker (1942)
Harry Rosin
Limestone on granite base

The Birth of a Nation (1943)
Henry Kreis
Limestone on granite base

The Revolutionary Soldier (1943)
and *The Statesman (1943)*
Erwin Frey
Limestone on granite bases

The theme is the representation of
the settlement of the East Coast
and the growth of democracy.

NORTH TERRACE

The Preacher (1952)
Waldemar Raemisch
Granite on granite base

The Poet (1954)
José de Creeft
Granite on granite base

The Scientist (1955)
Khoren Der Harootian
Granite on granite base

The Laborer (1958)
Ahron Ben-Shmuel
Granite on granite base

Eye and Hand (Relief Panels) (1959)
J. Wallace Kelly
Limestone on granite base

The theme is the spiritual forces
that developed the country.

63

Now we hike along the path once more and see across from us a horse stopped suddenly by his cowboy rider.

Bronze
Height: 12'
Base: poured concrete

Kelly Drive, north of Girard Avenue Bridge
Installed 1908

The Cowboy

FREDERIC REMINGTON

In 1880, at the age of 19, Frederic Remington went west to seek his fortune. His plan was to return to New England with enough money to be able to marry his sweetheart, Eva Caten. Out West he worked on wagon trains with cowboys and Indians, and he recorded this rough, hard life by drawing lots of sketches. After two years, he brought these vivid scenes of the last frontier to New York City and tried to sell them to publishers. Although he sold one to *Harper's Weekly* for ten dollars, he struggled for three more years before a friend at *Outing* magazine published his work. Then, suddenly, the public responded and he was in great demand by national magazines and for book illustrations. In one book alone, a special edition of Longfellow's *Hiawatha*, there were 400 of his illustrations. Soon there were Remington reproductions in homes across the nation. He had become the pictorial historian of the Old Wild West. In addition, he devoted much of his time to painting.

After Remington went down to Cuba as a correspondent in the Spanish-American War, he painted the famous *Charge of the Rough Riders at San Juan Hill*, a picture, it is said, that helped put Teddy Roosevelt in the White House.

However, it was the depiction of horses that most challenged and inspired him. Remington said that his epitaph should read, "He knew the horse." His first attempt at sculpture, *The Bronco Buster*, was so successful that his 250 bronze replicas were not enough to fill the demand for them. He portrayed the horse in about 25 bronze statues, all showing violent action. His joking ambition was to cast a bronco with all four feet off the ground.

When Remington came to Philadelphia to select a site for *The Cowboy*, he posed a horse and rider on the rock that now serves as the base for the sculpture. The model he used for the rider was a friend of his, Charlie Trego, who was born in Pennsylvania, went out west to become a cowboy and eventually became the manager of Buffalo Bill's Wild West Show. At the dedication of this statue, a famous scout called Wyoming Jack led a group of cowboys and Native American men in full warpaint (accompanied by their wives and children) to join the thousands of spectators along the East River Drive. Wyoming Jack and He-Dog, a Native American medicine man, unveiled *The Cowboy*. They were assisted by two members of the Children's Art Brigade, a group that had been established by the Fairmount Park Art Association in 1897 to encourage young people to participate in ceremonial events. Remington, however, did not attend. In a letter to the Art Association, he wrote, "No one pays much attention to the sculptor."

The Cowboy was the first and last large-size bronze by Remington because a year after it was installed he died after having an appendix operation. He was 48 years old. In just 25 years of creative work, he did illustrations for 142 books. He produced some 2,800 paintings and drawings and sculpted 25 bronzes.

64

After another long walk we come to another general on a horse. The model for this horse was a 19-year-old gray gelding that was sired by the Arabian stallion that the Sultan of Turkey had given to Grant in 1878.

Bronze
Height: 14′6″
Base: granite (16′4″)
One and a half times lifesize

Kelly Drive at Fountain Green Drive
Installed 1897

General Ulysses S. Grant

DANIEL CHESTER FRENCH AND EDWARD C. POTTER

General Grant was commander-in-chief of the Union Army in the Civil War. After the war he was made a full general, the first U.S. citizen to hold that rank since George Washington. After serving briefly as Secretary of War under President Andrew Johnson, he ran for office himself and became the 18th president of the United States. Having served two terms, he retired from the White House and spent two years making a triumphal tour around the world. When Grant returned and moved to New York City, he invested his money in a banking business that collapsed and left him bankrupt. In order to provide for his family, he tried writing and found he had talent. He wrote his final work while ill with throat cancer and he finished it four days before he died. It was called the *Personal Memoirs of U. S. Grant*, a book that Mark Twain had been eagerly waiting to publish. It became a popular success, bringing his heirs nearly $450,000. This two-volume work is considered to be among the great military narratives of history.

After Grant died, the Fairmount Park Art Association gave Daniel Chester French the commission to create a memorial. He asked Edward C. Potter to be his collaborator because Potter specialized in animal sculpture and this work was to be an equestrian statue.

French had invented a machine to help him enlarge his small models. It allowed him to work six to ten times faster. In the museum that was French's studio is a six-foot plaster model of Abe Lincoln that was a study for the 28-foot seated figure of Lincoln in the Lincoln Memorial in Washington, D.C. This model is considered to be a work of art on its own merits. It presents Lincoln, the man, rather than a figure of veneration.

In the span of his career, French left many well-known landmarks in dozens of U.S. cities, but *The Minute Man*, which he carved at the age of 25, and the Lincoln Memorial figure, which he finished 45 years later, are the highlights of his fame.

65

Near the river across from General Grant are three musical angels.

Bronze
Height: 7′
Bases: aggregate concrete (20′–23′)

Kelly Drive at Fountain Green Drive
Installed 1972

Playing Angels

CARL MILLES

Carl Milles, the sculptor of these musical angels, was born in Logga, Sweden, and when he was 17 years old, he went to Stockholm to be an apprentice to a cabinet maker. There he also studied at night at the Technical School. At the age of 22, he left for Paris and studied at the École des Beaux Arts and with Pierre Puvis de Chavannes and Antoine Louis Barye, all the while working at minimal jobs for survival. Milles became an assistant to Auguste Rodin and also studied in Munich, Germany. During his long career, his work varied and he developed his own fantasy style. In Stockholm, he opened a studio called the Millesgarden, which became a museum for his work. His reputation in Scandinavia was widespread and he received many public commissions. In 1913, at the Malmo Exhibition, he had an entire gallery devoted to his sculpture.

In 1930, Milles settled in the United States and began teaching at the Cranbrook Academy of Art in Bloomfield Hills, Michigan. His monuments, heroic figures, fountains and memorials are found in New York City; St. Paul, Minnesota; Chicago, London, Paris and in many cities in Sweden. Milles became an American citizen in 1945, but when he retired in 1953, he returned to Sweden. He died there in 1955 at the age of 80.

Each angel is playing a horn instrument. These sculptures are three of the five casts made from the five original angels, which are still playing in the Millesgarden overlooking the harbor in Stockholm.

66

Now there is quite a long walk or drive past the boat race stands to see the John B. Kelly Memorial.

Bronze
Height: 4′10″
Base: polished black granite on a brick footing (3′)

Kelly Drive near the Rowing Grandstand, just north of the Columbia Avenue railroad bridge
Installed 1965

John B. Kelly (The Rower)

HARRY ROSIN

John B. Kelly Sr. (1889–1960), who was one of America's greatest oarsmen, was denied entry in 1920 to the great gentlemen's sporting event, the Royal Henley Regatta, because he had worked with his hands. In 1947, his son, John B. Kelly Jr., went to that sculling classic on the Thames River in England and redeemed the snub to his father by winning the Henley. The senior Kelly was not only an Olympic oarsman, but a successful brick contractor and civic leader. He was the Democratic Party's candidate for mayor of Philadelphia in 1931. His daughter, the late Grace Kelly, was a famous actress who married the Prince of Monaco; and his brother, George Kelly, was a Broadway playwright and stage actor. His son, the late John B. Jr., was also active in Philadelphia politics, serving as a city councilman. A group of Kelly's friends suggested that a statue be designed in his memory, and contributions were accepted for this memorial. The Philadelphia Art Commission searched for an appropriate site for the sculpture. To assist them they used a composition board mock-up of the statue prepared by Harry Rosin, the sculptor. They moved the model to different locations to see how it could be viewed from the river and the road. They chose a place near the Schuylkill River's reviewing grandstand and the finish line where Kelly had won many races during the 1920s. It is located halfway between the bank of the river and the scenic highway that was named after him.

The sculpture presents a young rower seated with both hands on the oars in an artistically foreshortened single scull. It rests on a black granite pedestal that sits on a surface foundation of red bricks, the Kelly trademark. The statue was unveiled by Kelly's widow, Margaret, at ceremonies attended by Mayor James H. J. Tate and other city leaders on June 26, 1965.

Harry Rosin, a sculptor, architect and teacher, was born in Philadelphia and later lived in New Hope, Pennsylvania. He studied at the Philadelphia Museum School of Industrial Art, at the Pennsylvania Academy of the Fine Arts and in Paris. He exhibited widely and received medals, prizes and grants. From 1939 on, he taught sculpture and drawing at the Pennsylvania Academy of the Fine Arts.

CREDITS

All photographs by Roslyn F. Brenner except for the following:

The Benjamin Franklin Parkway
(courtesy of the Office of the City Representative)

John Christian Bullitt, Matthias William Baldwin, The North Pediment, The Amazon, The Lion Fighter, Swann Memorial Fountain
(courtesy of the Philadelphia Art Commission)

William Penn
(courtesy of the Free Library of Philadelphia, Print and Picture Collection)

Rocky
(courtesy of the *Philadelphia Inquirer*)